God, Your Money and You

Bryce Bartruff

CROSSLINK
PUBLISHING

God, Your Money and You

CrossLink Publishing
www.crosslink.org

ISBN 978-1-936746-02-6

Other books by this author:

Become the Person You're Meant To Be
Christian Focus Publications

Here Am I Send Me
College Press

A Pocket Guide to the Sayings of Jesus
Bethany House Publisher

Insight: Uncommon Sense for Common People
Bethany House Publishers

Endorsements

"Control of personal finances is a widespread concern. Debt, struggling to make ends meet, charitable giving - these are very real challenges for most people. Bryce Bartruff is a wise and knowledgeable guide, and I heartily recommend this book for its biblical and practical help."

Dr. Philip G. Ryken
President
Wheaton College

I am totally impressed with this book, it is a 'must read' for financially challenged people. Sometimes it takes a global financial crisis to alert us to the sheer irresponsibility or plain inability many of us display in relation to our personal finances. Most of us need help from time to time to properly steward the resources God gives us. Bryce Bartruff has served the church well and done us all a favor in pointing us to the biblical principles and common grace wisdom which can help us to be fiscally fit!

Dr. Liam W. Goligher
Senior Pastor, Tenth Presbyterian Church
Philadelphia, PA

"Bryce Bartruff has a strong track record of helping men and women gain control of their personal finances. I highly recommend this book.

Ridge Burns, D.Min
Executive Director
InFaith

In his book, Bryce Bartruff offers some simple but powerful advice on controlling personal finances. This is an excellent book that can easily be used in financial counseling.

Ronald W. Ferner
Dean, School of Business and Leadership
Cairn University

This is good stuff! The principles Bryce teaches are biblical, practical, and they work! Many people who found themselves in financial difficulty found a way out and now handle their finances in wise and productive ways. This material is much needed and if applied can help people to reverse their financial bondage and grow spiritually.

Cora Hogue-Koop
Former pastoral assistant at Tenth Presbyterian Church,
Philadelphia PA.

Bryce has done careful study with writing this book. He logically moves us through the basics of budgeting and prioritizing to the place of victorious giving. This book is more than an aid to personal finances. It is a biblically based adventure in living by faith in our Lord Jesus Christ, trusting Him to supply all our needs. It is a plan for faithful giving. I highly recommend this book for private reading as well as a textbook on finances.

Lawrence Wilkes, Ph.D.
Interim Senior Pastor, Crystal Cathedral
President, California Graduate School of Theology
Garden Grove, California

A helpful guide for the young couple starting off life together - to help them "begin and keep" their finances in order. Scriptural references were well chosen and interpreted soundly. It is a solid book on finances.

Jim Jessup
Director of Church Relations
WILLIAM JESSUP UNIVERSITY

Special Thanks

Special thanks to my father, Rev. Bryce Oliver Bartruff, whose life and ministry have been the inspiration for mine, to my wife Kathy who collaborated with me in navigating the challenges of life, to my sister Mary Horton who lives out the principles in this transcript, to Cora Hogue-Koop whose encouragement led to the formation of my seminars and ultimately this book, to Ron Ferner for his assistance with the chapter on ethics, and to the thousands of students who have sat through my seminars providing the motivation to make this book as practical and helpful as possible.

Forward

It is a contradiction that goes on generation after generation. The Bible talks about few subjects more than it does money, yet the church is relatively reticent and silent on the topic. The surrounding culture is talking about money all the time, yet with little of the practical wisdom that Scripture contains.

We seem to think that talking candidly about money is somehow unspiritual; yet it is the God we worship who has sovereignly decided to place us in a world where money, business, budget, commerce, and finances are an unavoidable dimension of everyone's life. So, God warns us of money's allure and its danger,, but he doesn't stop there, he also takes the time, in his Word, to tell you how to guard your heart and how to practically steward your resources. Yet many, many Christians lack financial understanding and practical training on how to think about and steward their God-given resources. This sets them up for a life of unwise decisions, inter-personal stress and long-term and debilitating debt. Not only do they give way to the constant temptations of a materialistic culture, they are also unable to participate freely in the work of God's kingdom, because they are too busy working to avoid the demise of debt. All of this is a spiritual crisis for the church of Jesus Christ that does not get the attention that it so desperately deserves.

So, it is wonderful to have a book that sits right in the center of a biblical worldview, that is unashamedly honest about all things financial and that offers you both concrete insight and steps to take that can alter your world of money forever. Bartruff does not leave any stones unturned and yet while being thorough and practical, he never forgets that all that we have belongs first and foremost to the Lord.

Like diet books, there are many fad money books out there. They offer novel insights and the hope of rapid change, but they seldom give you either. This book isn't one of them. It is rooted in the ancient wisdom of Scripture and bows its knee to the Creator, and because it does, it offers you help that has stood and will stand the test of time.

So, don't read this book. No, live with it. You will do well to labor patiently over each of its practical exercises. Open your heart and your bank account and let God use this book to change you and the way you think about and use money. And may you not only celebrate the freedom of living with money in God's wise way and be led to a deeper appreciation of his wisdom and his provision, but finally be led to better serve the one who is God's ultimate gift, his Son, the Lord Jesus Christ.

Dr. Paul David Tripp
President, Paul Tripp Ministries
Executive Director, Center for Pastoral Life and Care

TABLE OF CONTENTS

INTRODUCTION

It seems that everyone has financial challenges at some point in their life. You are no exception. After all, you picked up this book for a reason. Looking for answers is the first step in gaining control over your personal finances. Gaining knowledge about your money and learning how to use this knowledge to make wise decisions is, as some of my younger friends say, "huge." No one can promise you financial success, but there are basic principles and tools you can use to achieve your financial dreams. My goal is to help you establish a perspective of finances that will allow you to take the actions necessary to make your dreams of financial health and stability a reality. As a result, this publication is intended to be very practical. Each chapter contains principles, no-nonsense tools, and thoughtful exercises you can adapt to your personal circumstances. We will discuss how to remove the stress that typically results in family arguments; fun approaches for removing debt while at the same time pulling your family closer together; and how you can accumulate enough wealth to qualify as a millionaire – all this while maintaining a wholesome lifestyle.

You will find that the concepts taught in this book on personal finance are universal. They are consistent with the financial standards established over time, but fine-tuned to meet the practical objectives of this book. They are also presented in a way you can easily understand, quickly implement, and be inspired to apply to your individual circumstances for the foreseeable future. The premise of this book is that financial decisions should be made based on Christian values that include the highest of ethical standards. Psalms 24:1 reads, "The earth is the LORD's and the fullness thereof, the world and those who dwell therein." (ESV) If God is the owner of all and allows us to manage what is his, then it is our responsibility to make wise financial decisions.

This book is interactive. In order to profit most from this material, you need to read each chapter, think about the principles and tools provided, and determine how to apply them most effectively in your life. Discussion questions and exercises provide the opportunity to think through the rationale behind the information. They can be especially helpful if you form an Accountability Group through your church, Bible study group, community center, or circle of friends. Use the guidelines below to formulate your team. Together, you can discuss the material and hold one another accountable to complete the exercises each week. Stay with the book and focus on implementing the principles. As a result, you should gain a firm understanding of how to control your finances and incorporate the concepts into your life and be free from the stress that oppresses so many individuals and couples.

Do note: Please, write in this book! Consider it a tool to help you gain control over your personal finances. Jot notes in the columns, write thoughts in the margins, and underline or highlight sections that you may want to refer to later. Make copies of the various forms throughout, populating them with your personal information. When you have finished reading the material and completing the exercises, you should have in your possession your own personalized guidebook upon which you can continue to build and fine-tune your financial future.

Feel free to email me if you have specific questions, or would like to arrange a workshop on personal finance for your church or other organization.

GUIDELINES FOR ESTABLISHING A "FINANCIAL ACCOUNTABILITY TEAM"
Setting right priorities, getting out of debt, staying out of debt and otherwise managing personal finances is a difficult process. It requires, change in the way a person thinks about money, implementation of different spending patterns, a new approach to choices, and a focus on the discipline that brings financial health over the destructive behavior

associated with immediate gratification. Financial fitness, like a weight reduction diet is most effective when done with the support and encouragement of others. It is much better to tackle the money monster in concert with an Accountability Partner or an Accountability Team that provides direction and checks to see that you remain on track in achieving personal goals, than to try this on your own.

An Accountability Team is an assembly of people who meet regularly (weekly or bi-weekly) to review the discussion questions at the end of each chapter. They discuss budgets, spending patterns, investment decisions, debt reduction, personal struggles, communication issues and hold one another responsible for reaching individual objectives. An Accountability Partner is an individual who plays the same role but the relationship is one-on-one rather than team oriented. Some Accountability Teams consist of a group of Accountability Partners who come together to discuss their progress.

Here are some guidelines for starting and maintaining an Accountability Team/Partnership:

1. Agree to be accountable to one another for a specific period of time. This may be for a period as short as ten weeks or as long as twelve months. Establish a cut off date at which time you will reexamine your progress and determine if there is a need to renew your commitment.
2. Establish the parameters of this partnership including specific objectives, the frequency of meetings, structure of your time together, and length of meetings.
3. If you need help finding someone to be part of your accountability group, ask the leaders of your church to help. They are often aware of members of the congregation who want to improve their finances.
4. Use this textbook to get started. Cover no more than one chapter per week, completing the exercises and discussion questions you deem appropriate to your needs, together. Meeting weekly with an

accountability group with high standards of accountability can truly change a person's life.

5. Be honest and transparent with one other. Allow participants to share openly their feelings, frustrations, struggles and setbacks. Be tough on one another, expecting realistic goals and adherence to the supportive timelines.

6. Get the input of other group members before making any major purchases. Discuss temptations during your regular weekly meetings and call an Accountability Partner on the phone when enticed to buy a non-budgeted item. As you work through the discipline of debt reduction, setting right priorities, managing your money and investing for the future, keep your eyes on the goal. Being financially fit is healthy and biblical and pays tremendous lifetime dividends.

Chapter 1: God's Financial Plan for Your Life

The Bible has a great deal to say about God's financial plan for your life. Many of Christ's parables deal directly with values, priorities and money. Close examination reveals that more is said about money and possessions than about heaven and hell, and five times more is said about possessions and values than prayer. Why is such a great emphasis placed in this area? When asking this question of my audiences, someone almost always quotes Matthew 6:21, *"Where your treasure is, there will your heart be also"* (ESV). Because our hearts and our money are so closely related, the Scriptures contain guidelines designed to help us keep our priorities correct. As a result, we learn how to place God at the center of life and to look to Him for guidance. *He* is to be the treasure in life.

The first question and response in the Westminster Shorter Catechism provides a clear answer to why man exists. The question is asked, *"What is the chief end of man?"* The answer is *"Man's chief end is to glorify God, and to enjoy him forever."* If our goal is to enjoy God, we will look to the instruction book He has provided for us, that being the Bible to learn how this can be done. When biblical principles form the base of our decisions, then anxiety about future finances, the overwhelming pressures of debt, and the lack of time for family, sports, hobbies, church and other areas that should be priorities, will disappear. As a result, life can be focused on enjoying and glorifying God.

Imagine you were to die tonight. The pastor performing your eulogy would want to know about you and what your priorities really were. There is one place he could go to gain a reflection of where your priorities truly lay. This place is your checkbook or bank statement. Why? Financial records reveal your true values. People spend their money on the things that are of most importance to them. If the bulk of your current spending is on education, a mortgage, a car, food, children, vacations, recreation, clothes, dining out or a vacation home, then it is likely that these things are of greatest importance. If little or no money is spent in one of these areas, it is likely to be of little value to you.

A few years ago a young lady in my friend Bob's Adult Singles' Sunday school class asked him, a certified public accountant, if he would help her balance her checkbook. He agreed and during their time together was impressed by how well she had maintained her checkbook and the depth of her questions. Later, as he reflected on where she spent her money, he thought to himself, "*It is a person with these priorities that I would like to have as my wife.*" This prompted his pursuit to build a long-term relationship with her. Within a year, they were married.

I encourage you to take some time today to look at your bank statements. Where are you spending the bulk of your money? Does your bank statement reflect where you would like it to be spent? If the pastor doing your eulogy were to use your financial statements as a basis for determining what is truly important to you, would he find what you would like him to see? What changes do you need to make in your spending in order for you to be satisfied?

A scriptural perspective of money and priorities is seen in a parable Jesus told in Luke 12:16-21. It reads as follows:

> *[16] And he told them a parable, saying, "The land of a rich man produced plentifully, [17] and he thought to himself 'What shall I do, for I have nowhere to store my crops?' [18] And he said, 'I will do this: I will tear down my barns and build larger ones, and there I will store all my grain and my goods. [19] And I will say to my soul, "Soul, you have ample goods laid up for many years; relax, eat, drink, be merry." ' [20] But God said to him, 'Fool! This night your soul is required of you, and the things you have prepared, whose will they be?' [21]* **So is the one who lays up treasure for himself and is not rich toward God.**"

What this man decided to do with his newfound wealth caused God to give him a "death sentence." Some people, in reflection on this parable, say he was just making the decision to retire, that is, to stop working as he had enough goods to supply what he needed for the rest of his life. "What" they ask, "is wrong with retirement?" Actually, what he chose to do was very different than traditional retirement. He demonstrated an intense level of selfishness, by only thinking about himself. He did not indicate he would take his good fortune and spend time at the local synagogue studying the scriptures so he could learn more about God, or teaching others how to be more productive, or even spending more time with his children. No, his thoughts were selfish, centered upon himself and himself alone. He focused on what would provide immediate, self-gratification; not on how he could be of service to his family, his community or God.

The purpose of this parable is to help us learn from the error of this selfish, rich man and fix our minds on those things that will have lasting value. We should focus on that which will bring true inner peace, happiness, and satisfaction. We should not store up for ourselves things that just bring immediate gratification, but instead seek to become spiritually rich, setting our priorities on the things that will glorify God. Our focus should not be on ourselves and the possessions and lifestyle we can gain for ourselves. Instead, the thrust of our lives, including how we spend our money, should have a foundation in Biblical principles and the priorities God would have for our lives. This shift in precedence will be reflected in how we gain and spend our money. Its evidence will be seen in our checkbooks and bank statements, the way we spend our time and how we cultivate relationships within our family.

One of our goals should be to place ourselves in a position where we can concentrate our time and effort on the things that should be important in life, a place where we won't be anxious about money. In the pages ahead we will explore how to set ourselves up for financial success so that we have the appropriate balance in life, and so that the amount of money we possess is not a burden but a blessing. This is the "worry-free" lifestyle that God intends for us. Note the Scripture below:

> [25] *"Therefore I tell you, do not be anxious about your life, what you will eat or what you will drink, nor about your body, what you will put on. Is not life more than food, and the body more than clothing?* [26] *Look at the birds of the air: they neither sow nor reap nor gather into barns, and yet your heavenly Father feeds them. Are you not of more value than they?* [27] *And which of you by being anxious can add a single hour to his span of life? Matthew 6:25-27*

The birds of the air do not need to worry about anything. However, my friend Kerri has pointed out sarcastically, "Birds just fly around and sing songs. God makes a nest for them and they move into the nest, sit in their recliner, and watch their big-screen HD or 3DTV. God drops food into their nest when it is needed. Right? Since this verse says God provides for his children, we are entitled to this same kind of treatment. All we need to do is to sit at home and pray, waiting for God to send us all the luxuries and food we desire."

Kerri, while being cynical, was trying to make an important point. God does provide birds the means by which to live and to provide for their offspring. This centers on their instinct and desire to do the work that allows them to survive. The early bird is up first thing in the morning gathering twigs and mud; and those in the city even find building material such as Styrofoam and string to build a nest. Once their nest is built, birds begin work early every day gathering insects and worms to feed their families. They smartly build their nests in an environment that allows them to protect their family from danger and they teach their chicks to fly. God gives them the resources needed to build a healthy family including time, ability and resources, and they are expected to do their part by using these resources to thrive. When they do their part, they are able to live without the need to worry. Thus, the parable about "worry free" birds.

We, too, are to use the resources God has given to us. In the process of doing our part we are able to live "worry free" lives in the financial sense. We have been provided with an assortment of tools we often take for granted. One of the most important of these tools is our intelligence. As human beings, we have learned how to work together to design and build houses that keep us safe from harsh outdoor elements, to acquire food in large quantities, and clothes far and above what we minimally need. We have also learned to acquire extras, such as transportation, health care, jewelry, recreation, hobbies and even electronic entertainment. In order to take advantage of the systems in our society that allow for financial health, we need to position ourselves so that we are able to provide for ourselves and our families in a balanced and healthy way. This includes learning how to acquire and then manage money.

Just like the birds, when we learn to work hard, consistently and wisely, we can put worry behind us. This requires getting out of bed each day and going to our job or place of business. When we are out of work, we need to do our part by finding employment, regardless of how humble, or starting our own businesses. God provides unlimited opportunities in our society for even the most modest of people. Few people in our culture actually starve or live without shelter unless they have psychological illnesses or have made a conscious decision to be homeless. The Lord provides the opportunities, but just like the birds, we are expected to do our part in the process. We are given the freedom to work hard so we can make the most of the opportunities that come our way (Ephesians 5:15-16) or to do nothing and reap the natural results of our laziness.

The scriptures teach, *"The earth is the Lord's and the fullness thereof, the world and those who dwell therein,"* Psalms 24:1. If we understand that God owns all things and our role is to develop what He has given to us for His glory, then we take on a refreshing perspective of life. If he is the owner of all and we are responsible to manage the things he has entrusted to us, we will take seriously our responsibility to work hard and smartly to develop the resources of time, opportunity, and knowledge to build a lifestyle for ourselves and for our family that honor our Lord. Hard work and wise decisions allow us to reap the same benefits as the birds of the air – a life free from worry about financial things. The intent of this book is to help readers understand how to establish healthy priorities and manage money in a way that allows them to live worry free.

Priorities

Personal priorities influence the decisions we make in managing money. Linda was distraught. Her uncle Frank had just died. "We are all really going to miss him," she said. "He was so gentle, thrifty, and generous. In fact, his generosity is reflected in his inheritance. He left my husband, Bob, and me $150,000." The money was in a tax-free trust, so Linda and Bob would be able to use all of the money for anything they desired. They were trying to figure out how to best use their inheritance. Bob wanted to purchase a boat, but Linda wanted to put $15,000 toward a super-spending spree, put some toward a new car, and invest the rest for retirement.

Linda's sister, Mary, and her husband, Loren, received the same generous gift. They, too, were determining the best way to spend the money. Mary was eager to give 15% to her church and to missions. She also wanted to have a memorable vacation in Europe, pay off her credit cards, and retire their mortgage. It was hard for both couples to know the right decisions to make.

Not everyone receives a large gift of cash, but thinking through the possibilities of what you might do with such a gift provides a sense of what is important to you. I have asked dozens of couples to complete an exercise in which they imagine what they would do if they received $150,000 tax-free. Without looking at the answers of their partners, they privately list how they think they would spend the money. After completing the exercise, they share their conclusions with one another. Sometimes the answers are similar. Often they are very different.

Decisions on where to spend money reveal a great deal about the personal priorities and potential problems a couple may have in their relationship. The person who immediately expresses a desire to give a large gift to the church or missions is on a different path from their spouse if their spouse is only thinking of immediate personal gratification. Our individual perspectives of the world and where we are in our movement through life play greatly upon the financial decisions we make.

People who understand what is important to them at this point in their life will have an easier time setting spending priorities and making decisions. With little trouble they can determine where to spend their money, how to allocate their time, and where to focus their energies. Questions for you to consider include "Do you spend the majority of your time and energy trying to have fun, partying, and hanging out with friends? Or are you focused on working and securing opportunities to gain more money? Do you purchase only the best quality products or the least expensive? Do you desire to put as much money as you can in the bank and toward investments? Is it important for you to be involved in church, community service, and politics? These questions address the issue of where you desire to invest your time and spend your money. It reveals a great deal about who you are as an individual.

If you take the time to identify what your priorities are, you will have meaningful criteria with which to make financial decisions. If, for example, spending time with family is highly important then time spent at work will take a lesser priority. It will be acceptable to have fewer possessions and a lifestyle that is somewhat austere so you can be with your family. If, on the other hand, spending money on a lavish lifestyle is highly important, time spent with family will need to be a lesser priority. It will be acceptable to have fewer hours with them in order to gain the money to own more things. A former Deacon at my home church chose to step away from a promising career in one of the nation's top accounting firms. He indicated that he made the decision to work for a small company at a lower pay because of what he saw in the lives of the partners who worked for his firm. Each partner worked an excessively large number of hours weekly and each had experienced at least one divorce as a result. He asked himself, "What am I trying to accomplish?" The answer was that he wanted to build his relationship with his wife and to raise godly children. In order to reach this objective, he needed to forgo a high income and focus a balanced allotment of time and attention on his wife and children.

Another friend, Bill, was an executive with a large, international company. Most weeks he flew to cities throughout the world and returned home on the weekend. This lifestyle fit him and his wife, Carol, well as she is deeply involved in her own activities and their children were grown. Bill and Carol live in a modest home, and, as a result, have paid off their house and can contribute large sums of money to their church and to missions. They have consciously made the decision to forego an elegant home, luxurious vacations and expensive clothes and gadgets. As a result, they have more than they need and are in control of their finances. Their finances are not in control of them. As a couple, they made the decision to become missionaries to university students in China. Unencumbered by financial obligations, the decision was made without concern for finances. They were able to move into a new era of life when the opportunity presented itself. We each need to consciously decide on the balance that is right for us at this point in our lives. After all, the decisions we make about time and money are based on our priorities. Once we have a healthy understanding of our personal goals we can focus on establishing the lifestyle we believe God has in mind for us.

Consider the decisions Linda and Mary faced when they received $150,000 tax-free from their Uncle Frank. Imagine yourself in their place. Take a few minutes and write down how you would spend this money if you were to receive it today. Would you pay off your credit cards, go on a spending spree, take a wonderful vacation, purchase a new home, or give money to your favorite charity or spend it in other ways? Space is provided in the Discussion Questions and Assignments section at the end of this chapter for you to list how you would spend this money. If you are married, have your spouse engage in this same exercise.

After you have had an opportunity to write down how you would spend your financial gift, take a few minutes and ask yourself what these choices reveal about what is important to you. Did your list dwell predominantly on debt reduction, physical pleasure, care for your family, charity, missions, your church, your home, transportation, vacation, or education? There is no correct universal answer that best fits everyone. We each are at different stages of life and have a unique set of interests, circumstances, and goals for the future. There are, however, some priorities that are not healthy and that will lead to future financial and personal ruin. A strong focus on personal gratification, the desire to purchase more possessions instead of paying off obligations, and the intent not to share with others but to spend solely on oneself are problematic (Luke 12:16-21). On the other hand, individuals who desire to develop the self-discipline needed to pay off their debts and to share with others are those who are able to sleep well at night, with minimal anxiety.

Establishing God's financial plan for your life requires the willingness to look at the world from His perspective. What principles has He provided in the scriptures that guide you to an understanding of what He would have you do with your money? What kind of a lifestyle does He desire for you? Until now, He has provided you, His child, with sufficient resources. Learning to live with what may seem to you to be limited wealth, may be frustrating. But giving up your desire for more than He desires and resting in the provision He has provided without becoming anxious, will bring inner peace. This does not mean you cannot seek a better lifestyle or more things. It is, however, a conscious decision to turn your money and lifestyle over to God, and to trust in Him for direction as to what is best for you. This is not easy for most people, but, once it is achieved, the blessings of inner peace and the close relationship with Him that results are well worth the struggle.

God wants you to live in a manner that brings you financial health. Proverbs 30: 8 and 9 read *Remove far from me falsehood and lying; give me neither poverty nor riches; feed me with the food that is needful for me,* ^{9} *lest I be full and deny you and say, "Who is the LORD?" or lest I be poor and steal and profane the name of my God."* Here, the emphasis is on balance. The author is asking God to provide for him exactly what he needs in order to live a balanced life. People who have too much often fail to appreciate what the Lord has done for them and take their blessing for granted. They soon forget from whom their blessings come. Conversely, people who do not have enough upon which to sustain life are tempted to turn from their moral judgments and steal. The wise person will pray to the Lord, asking to be given exactly what they need. As we move through life, it is important that we recognize that God controls all things, including our life circumstances. To be appreciative of this is proper indeed. In Psalms 139:16 we are reminded that each of our days were charted out for us, even before we were born. This being so, it is our responsibility to accept our circumstances, making the best of them. Ephesians 5:16 instructs us to *"make the most of every opportunity."* Again in II Corinthians 8:7 we are instructed *"But as you excel in everything – in faith, in speech, in knowledge, in all earnestness, and in our love for you – see that you excel in this act of grace also."* Making the best of our circumstances and seeking excellence need to be sought and cultivated in the life of every believer. Luke 16: 10-12 points to the importance of understanding what it is that we have been given and that we have the responsibility to develop these things for the glory of God. Verses 10 through 12 read, ^{10} *"One who is faithful in a very little is also faithful in much, and one who is dishonest in a very little is also dishonest in much.* ^{11} *If then you have not been faithful in the unrighteous wealth, who will entrust to you the true riches?* ^{12} *And if you have not been faithful in that which is another's, who will give you that which is your own?"* True riches are of course not things; rather they are the intangible aspects of life. The possessions God puts into our lives are to be used properly and for His glory.

God has given you the skills and time needed to secure the money you need for the lifestyle He desires for you. What is often hard to accept is the quality of the lifestyle he has in mind for you at this point in time. Many people desire a lavish standard of living, but few will receive it. An extravagant lifestyle is not what life is all about. Our role as God's children is to accept our present situation, making the most of our circumstance so that our Lord is glorified. The Apostle Paul stated it brilliantly in Philippians 4:12 when he said, *"I know what it is to be in need, and I know what it is to have plenty. I have learned the secret of being* **content** *in any and every situation, whether well fed or hungry, whether living in plenty or in want."(NIV)* Paul led a life that has influenced millions of people over centuries of time. Our simple role is to take the resources God has given to us and develop a lifestyle we believe will be healthy for us. Do note that the Apostle Paul used the word "content". He did not use the word "satisfied". He was "content" in his current situation but was not "satisfied" with his circumstances. At the time he wrote this letter, he was in prison, and, as a Roman citizen, he appealed to Caesar for a hearing. He was content that he was where God would have him but he was not satisfied with his guilty verdict and imprisonment. He therefore did his part by pleading to be heard in a higher court.

Most people are able to change their standard of living over time. Our current circumstances may be very humble. Willingness to accept these circumstances for today will allow peace of mind. We can then evaluate what we should change to create an appropriate or improved standard of living for the future. Accepting where we are today will bring inner peace and contentment for today. Making plans for the future which is determining and making a commitment to the amount of time and effort we must spend to change our circumstances – provides hope.

If a person decides to change their current standard of living, they must be willing to do whatever is necessary to make that change. It may be, of course, that they will need to place a great deal of time on developing employable skills or working smarter so they are able to be positioned in a better work situation. They may need to gain an education in a specific area or develop a new skill set so employers want to hire them; or they may need to work longer hours in order to bring in more money. Conversely, they may decide to live a simple lifestyle focusing their time on non-work related activities. In making changes, we need to be aware of the impact our efforts will have on other areas of life. This balance of priorities, time and goals will need to be continually evaluated throughout life.

Seeking to understand what your priorities are today will provide an opportunity to determine if they should be changed or what you need to do to see that they become a reality. Priorities directly impact financial goals. Each person's financial needs are as unique as the person. DNA and fingerprints are specific to the individual. Your experiences, quality of friendships, dreams, and aspirations are unlike those of anyone else. God has a plan and purpose for each person that only they can fulfill. He has placed each person in a world in which they are allowed to secure and spend money within certain parameters, making decisions that are uniquely their own.

When we work within God's parameters and make decisions in a manner consistent with our faith, we can experience inner peace. Of course, if we choose to violate these parameters, frustration, anxiety, anger, bitterness, depression and wrong priorities may step in.

Our responsibility is to determine the focus of our life and make decisions that support that focus. This process is not always easy. Making long-term objectives can seem overwhelming. For many people it is best to make short-term goals based on a general understanding of the situation or lifestyle they believe God would have for them in the years ahead. Goals allow a person to determine the amount of money needed to set a direction for fulfilling financial priorities. Once immediate and long-term priorities are set, we will know what lifestyle is appropriate right now and in general where it should be in the future. We know the amount we should be saving; when it is appropriate to spend money on frivolity, gifts, and entertainment; how much debt (if any) we are comfortable with; how much time we should spend at work; the social activities in which we should engage; and even the amount of time and money we should designate to Christian endeavors.

With our priorities in line, we can make the conscious decision to alter spending patterns and make lifestyle changes in order to become free from the anxiety and tension associated with debt. Change is not always easy, especially change that requires a less lavish lifestyle. Yet, gaining control of our personal finances usually demands this type of change. If we want to own our home outright, pay cash for our cars, have sufficient money in the bank to retire, or enjoy a stress-free family life without arguments about finances, we must be willing to make the many changes necessary to meet these goals. Without looking at how to change spending patterns, our financial situation will not improve, and we likely will not achieve long-term wealth.

As Christians in a fairly free society, we have a great deal of influence over our income and need to act wisely to optimize our financial potential. That does not mean seeking to acquire as much wealth as possible. Rather, it means determining a standard of living we believe is right for us and taking the actions necessary to support that lifestyle. As mature Christians, life is not about how much material gain we can receive. It is about obtaining a lifestyle that we fully understand God has in mind for us. This forms the basis for establishing our financial plan and spending patterns.

Discussion Questions and Assignments:

1. Take some time today to look at your bank statements. Make a list of the four areas in which you are you spending the bulk of your money.

    _____   _____

    _____   _____

       A. What does this say to you about your priorities?
       B. Are you pleased with what you find?
       C. What changes would you like to make if any in your spending priorities?

2. Consider the decisions Linda and Mary faced when they received $150,000 tax free from their Uncle Frank. Imagine yourself in their place. Take a few minutes and write down how you would spend this money if you were to receive it today. Space is provided below for you to list how you would spend this money. If you are married, have your spouse engage in this same exercise.

	You		Your Spouse	
Item	Amount	Item	Amount	
_____	_____	_____	_____	
_____	_____	_____	_____	
_____	_____	_____	_____	
_____	_____	_____	_____	
_____	_____	_____	_____	
_____	_____	_____	_____	
_____	_____	_____	_____	

3. Now that you have had an opportunity to write down how you would spend your financial gift, explain what these choices reveal about what is important to you.

4. How should your response to question number 3 influence where you spend your time, effort, finances and priorities during the next 12 months?

5. In Philippians 4:12 we learn that we are to be content but, we are not instructed to be satisfied.

   A. How was this seen in the life of the Apostle Paul?
   B. How might this be displayed in your life or the life of someone close to you?

6. Establishing God's financial plan for your life requires the willingness to look at the world from His perspective. Describe below the kind of lifestyle God has in mind for you today based upon the resources you have at your disposal. How do you desire your lifestyle to change in the next 4 years? Use the space below to formulate your answers.

   A. Major areas where you spend your time

   Today:

   Four years from now:

   B. Major expenses

   Today:

   Four years from now:

C. Major areas of interest

Today:

Four years from now:

D. Home environment

Today:

Four years from now

7. Identify four things you need to do in the next 48 months in order to achieve the lifestyle you believe God would have for you to live four years from now?

8. Consider the story of the birds as found in Matthew 6:25-27. What personal implications does this have upon your life?

9. The first question and response in the Westminster Shorter Catechism provides a clear answer to why we are here on earth.
   A. What is the reason given?
   B. How might this influence the way you choose to spend money and the lifestyle you choose for yourself?

10. Some people measure their self-worth by the kind of car they drive, the clothes they wear, the neighborhood in which they live or the kind of recreational activities in which they engage. Contemplate your personal life. On a scale of 1 (lowest) to 10 (highest) rate the importance of each of the following items as to their importance to you. Add several of your own to the list:
    a. _____ Automobile
    b. _____ Clothes
    c. _____ Quality of home

d. _____ Social status of the people with whom you spend time
e. _____ Type of employment
f. _____ Recreation / hobby
g. _____ Status of your church or social club
h. _____ School you or your children attend or graduate from
i. _____ Kind of restaurants in which you eat
j. _____ _____
k. _____ _____
l. _____ _____

11. Consider carefully the items listed in the above exercise. How do these influence the financial decision you make? Are they consistent with the values of the other people in your immediate family or closest friends? How does this impact your discussions about finances?

12. Consider your personal lifestyle objectives.
    a. Ideally, what would you like your world to look like in three years, five years and ten years? Where would you like to live, what would your home look like, how would your diet, your recreational activities, your employment, your savings, and family make-up be different than it is today?
    b. Discuss your dreams with other members of your family and possibly your closest friends, especially your spouse. What are their insights about the life you envision?
    c. What would you need to do in order to make the changes in your lifestyle you believe are appropriate?
    d. List projected dates for completing the changes or goals you listed.

Chapter 2: Decision Making and Priorities

Arguments in marriages tend to fall into several major areas. Volatile topics for most couples include issues associated with childrearing, in-laws, sex, and of course, family finances. In fact, reportedly between 55 to 60 percent of arguments in the typical family have to do with money. A quick search on the internet indicates that in approximately 50% of divorces, finances play a major role, and in 90% of divorces, they are a contributing factor. This is significant. For many people, the frustrations associated with finances can seem overwhelming. Setting financial priorities, choosing what will be purchased, understanding the difference between lifestyle needs and desires, determining how to pay expenses, and deciding who is responsible to take care of bills can erupt to a level of intense conversation that tears a family apart. However, the couple who understands how to deal with these issues and seeks to understand God's financial plan for their lives will see these tensions dissipate. The process of setting priorities and communicating effectively is ongoing and sometimes difficult. When couples learn how to communicate effectively about their finances and work together toward common goals they reduce the stress and disruptive commotion in their lives. They find the subject of money pulls them together instead of tearing them apart. This is not generally an easy task. It is however an achievable objective.

One important aspect of avoiding marital tension about money is to learn how to discuss financial goals with one another. In order to accomplish this, couples need to follow several guidelines. 1) They should have regular discussions about family finances. This includes establishing both long and short-term goals. 2) They must be willing to take 15-30 minutes each week to manage their finances by paying bills. 3) They need to decide on their current and anticipated income levels and expenditures. They can then track them to see if they are in line with their priorities. 4) They should also pray together about financial decisions before they are made. Such a process requires discipline, time and effort. However, undertaking these four steps can be a fun process that draws a family closer together.

1) Discuss family finances: Life for most families is full of many activities and responsibilities. Sometimes the volume of activities can seem overwhelming. Employment, interacting with children, attending church activities and sports practice, completing dinner and wrapping up the ordinary activities of daily living can leave little time for thoughtful interaction. Decisions regarding financial matters can take a distant second to more pressing issues. For this reason, couples typically need to schedule a specific time during the week in which to discuss their budget, family goals and any financial issues they may be facing. The period of time may only be 15 minutes, but it needs to be a time designated exclusively for this purpose. This interaction may be after the children are in bed and in which the house is quiet, during a scheduled walk around the block, or during a weekly date where the couple is able to concentrate on their relationship with one another. The focus of the conversation is to address new or unexpected expenditures, potential new disbursements, outstanding bills, where the money will come from to meet obligations, who is responsible for making payments and determining how this will impact the total budget and family goals. Knowing a block of time is scheduled for this conversation allows the couple to set aside the tensions of finances until the designated appointment. People are freed from the need for spontaneous high-tension arguments when they recognize there is an avenue for issues to be addressed. Some couples are very organized, writing down issues during the week so they are sure to address them during their time together. It is not necessary that this is the only topic covered but the couple who has designated time together during which they can discuss family issues, including finances, will have in place a logical system for effective communication and problem solving. They can think carefully about their options, speak candidly about their concerns and discuss creative options openly.

2) Designate time to pay bills: "I hate paying the bills," grumbled Josh, as he complained about the financial situation he and his wife

Robin faced. Somehow the activities of daily living became overwhelming and little time was left to carry out the task of paying bills. Both Josh and Robin worked full-time, were involved with their church and were actively involved in their children's lives. In the bustle of activities some bills were not paid regularly, their bank balance was not always kept current, and this affected their credit score. Now, facing the prospect of purchasing a new home, they wanted to get the lowest interest rate possible on their mortgage. Periodic late payments led to a lower credit score than was ideal and this impacted the interest rate on their new mortgage and the amount of money they were able to borrow. How much different it would have been if they had employed the discipline necessary to designate a time each week in which to pay their bills. Carving out 15 - 30 minutes each week in which to focus on writing checks, making transfers and reconciling accounts is more than enough time for the typical family to spend in this area. It does require the discipline to schedule the time to make this happen, but the long-term ramifications are significant. Just as designating a specific time to discuss financial issues with your husband or wife takes discipline, designating a 15 - 30 minute period each week to pay bills requires effort. Making sure all bills are paid on time will impact a family's credit score, and will result in the reduction of family tension. When both parties can rest, knowing their finances are in order, it is well worth regulating the necessary effort.

3) Decide on realistic levels of income and expense: Many people desire to have more possessions than are appropriate for them based upon where they are in life's journey. The new college graduate should not expect to have the same level of wealth and possessions as the older person who has had the opportunity to receive a systematic increase in wages over many years. Other people may not have engaged in a career that will provide the level of income they desire. As a result, they may feel trapped, believing they are not able to secure the things they would like to possess. Sometimes such individuals become impatient. Instead of waiting until they have enough money to purchase the items they want, they place these items on their charge card. The result is the inability to pay for a lifestyle they cannot afford.

As they continue to charge items they go deeper and deeper into debt and begin to feel the pressure of their inability to pay their creditors. The resulting tension often causes them to become angry with their situation, frustrated with one another, irritated with themselves and mad at God.

In order to determine an appropriate spending level, each person needs to decide the role possessions will play in their life at this point in time. For some people, this is difficult because they base their identities on what they own. They judge their value as a person by the kind of car they drive, the quality of the clothes they wear, the kind of home they live in, the restaurants in which they eat or the type of recreation in which they engage. Those who place their identities not on things but on being a child of God and that alone, take on an entirely different perspective. The focus of their life is on their relationship with God. Things play a secondary role.

Just as the Apostle Paul had specific written goals, we too should have goals for the future and work to achieve these goals. At the same time, we need to rest in God, knowing He will get us through our current circumstances and help us to achieve our future goals. Families who set lifestyle objectives, determining what their life should be like in three years, ten years and even twenty year segments will be able to work together toward their mutually agreed upon goals. Lifestyle goals tend to draw a family together as they discuss them, and make the necessary decisions and changes in order to bring them into reality. Once lifestyle objectives are determined, then a couple can track their spending and income levels to see if they are on target.

If purchases exceed expenses, a simple deduction will conclude that either income needs to increase or expenses need to be reduced. Tracking and discussing progress in this area will allow a couple to make adjustments as needed.

4) Pray: Setting financial goals for life can seem overwhelming. As plans are prayerfully set, they need to be turned over to God looking to

Him for wisdom. At the same time we need to do our part by working systematically, consistently, and diligently toward our goals.

Proverbs 16:3, tells us to "Commit to the Lord whatever you do, and your plans will succeed" (NIV). We are to commit our plans to the Lord, turning them over to Him for His blessing. This includes our future financial and lifestyle goals. Of course, committing our plans to God presupposes certain parameters. Primarily, it assumes goals are God-centered. That is, they are based on His priorities, are supported by biblical principles, and are not selfish.

Once we have reviewed our goals to determine they do not contradict the teachings of the Scriptures, we should then bathe them in payer. The person who desires a new house, money to pay off debts, furniture, a vacation, new employment, development of new job skills, or even to achieve a completely different lifestyle should pray in detail and ask God for his blessing and direction.

My father, a missionary who started a number of churches in the Pacific Northwest, shared with me the premise of his prayers for the future. He said his prayer was, *"Lord, let my will be Your will."* He pointed out that God answers prayers in a positive way if what we ask for fits within the kind of request He desires to honor. When we pray, we should ask for things that are godly in nature and fit the priorities we find in the Bible. Selfish prayers based upon sinful desires will be hard pressed to receive the blessing and success we find in Proverbs 16:3. God focused prayer is an important part of establishing an appropriate lifestyle and spending patterns.

What Is Money and Who Owns It?

My friend Gary asked me an interesting question. He said, "I was reading the other day and found that I Timothy 6:10 says money is the root of all evil. But I work 60 hours or more a week to get money to buy my family the things I believe they need. Is it right to do that? If money is the root of all evil, maybe I should stop working to make money and forget the whole thing."

Together Gary and I turned to the scriptures and I read the passage out loud.

For the *love of money* is a *root* of all kinds of evil.
Some people, eager for money, have wandered from the
faith and pierced themselves with many griefs.
(I Timothy 6:10, NIV)

Gary had of course misread the scripture. A careful review of the verse revealed that money is not what is evil. Rather, it is the *love of money* that is a *root of all kinds of evil*. There is nothing inherently wrong with money itself. Money is simply a tool that allows us to provide for our family, purchase food, clothes, shelter, and transportation, and help the church minister to others. If Gary was motivated to work by the selfish desire to have an inappropriately lavish lifestyle, it may be he should cut back on his work hours. If he was following God's plan for his life and working out of love for his family and his desire to provide a healthy life for them, he was doing the right thing.

What money does is to "put us on the line" as to what our priorities really are. Why do we work? Where do we spend our money? Do we have the proper balance of activities in our life? The answers to these questions help us recognize what is truly important to us. Earning, investing, and spending money can all be done for the right reasons or because of the wrong motivation. We need to examine our motives to make sure our actions are in line with what God wants for us.

This is well illustrated in one of my favorite parables. In Matthew 25:14-30 Jesus tells the story of a man who, before going on a journey, called three of his servants to him and entrusted a certain amount of money to each. To one he gave five talents (one talent was worth approximately 20 years wages for the typical worker), to another he gave two talents, and to the third he gave one. He asked each servant to invest this money for him while he was away. Upon his return, the one to whom he had entrusted the five talents had doubled the investment. Upon seeing how well this servant did, the man rewarded the servant with added responsibilities and presumably financial rewards that matched his new responsibilities. The servant to whom he gave the two talents, likewise, doubled the investment and was also given greater responsibilities. The servant whom had been entrusted with the one talent was afraid of his master and did nothing with what he was entrusted. In fact, he dug a hole and hid the money in the ground so it would not be stolen. The master considered this act cowardly. It made him terribly angry. As a result the servant was punished severely.

The point of this parable is that God has given to each of us a variety of resources. We have a responsibility to develop and use these gifts for Him. We do not own these assets. God owns them. As is stated in Psalms 24:1, "The earth is the LORD's and the fullness thereof, the world and those who dwell therein." We are responsible to develop them for our Master. So, the question is: "What is it that God has entrusted to us?" The simple answer is that He has entrusted everything to us. That includes money, a physical presence, talent, our background, friends, family, relationships, knowledge, experiences, all of our possessions, and even our interests. God owns everything about us and in our possession. Our responsibility is to use it all for His honor and glory. We are just the caretakers. This concept should cause us to pause and think about the responsibility God has entrusted to us. After all, God owns us and everything about us. As His caretakers, we are to use all we have and are for His glory. He expects us to be responsible with what He has entrusted to us.

Take a few minutes to consider carefully all the things you are aware of that the Lord has entrusted to you. Use the form provided below titled "Deed of Possessions" to list as many of the things you can think of that God has blessed you with. At first the exercise may seem difficult, but as you begin thinking about your 1) possessions, 2) background, 3) areas of expertise, 4) relationships, 5) experiences, 6) passions, and 7) ambitions, your list will grow. Start by selecting each of these seven areas and list four or five items that fit each one. Soon you will find the page overflowing with what God has given to you to use for His glory.

Next, consider how each one of these gifts can be used for the glory of God. The impact any one person can make on the people in his or her circle of family and friends can be significant. Knowing we make a difference in the lives of those around us should have a positive influence on our behavior. We will have a different perspective on personal goals in general and on setting specific priorities for spending time and resources when we recognize all that the Lord has entrusted to us. Consider carefully the changes in behavior, amount of time spent working and type of spending you believe you should make in order to develop what God has entrusted to you. The person who believes their life is given to them by God to benefit others and ultimately to glorify God will spend their time and resources differently than the person who centers all behaviors on their personal needs and desires.

DEED OF POSSESSIONS

I hereby acknowledge God owns all that I have including my family, talents, time, ambitions and possessions. He has given me stewardship responsibilities for each of the following:

ITEM

_____   _____

_____   _____

_____   _____

_____   _____

_____   _____

_____   _____

_____   _____

_____   _____

_____   _____

_____   _____

_____   _____

_____   _____

_____   _____

_____   _____

_____   _____

Today's Date: _____ / _____ / _____

Signature of Recognition:

_____

The question is, "Does knowing that God really owns everything and we are caretakers of his possessions make a difference in how we spend money?" Of course it should. Recognizing who owns everything should cause us to think twice before spending money. After all, money is a tool owned by God, under our trust, to be used to glorify Him. We are not the end user – God is.

When you walk through the hardware store and see a wonderful drill on sale – a drill that you have been watching for months – or spot a special pair of shoes at the department store that will fit your wardrobe perfectly, ask yourself the ultimate question: "How will this purchase glorify my Lord?" It may be that the purchase is very appropriate. It may also be that the expense is very selfish and will put your budget out of balance because it is an expense that you have not planned for. Regardless, you need to keep in mind whom it is that owns the money you spend. You can then decide if it fits into His plan for your life. Life is not about us, and our enjoyment. Life is about serving the Lord and making purchases that are in His best interest.

One of the most significant areas in which people struggle is how to know when a purchase is appropriate. For many, they are torn between being miserly and not spending their money on an appropriate lifestyle and conversely, going overboard and spending too much. Three questions a person can ask that will help them make the right purchases are:

1. *Is it appropriate to use God's money in this way?* Does it seem to fit God's plan for how I should spend money at this point in time? Just because someone else feels the purchase is good does not mean that it fits within God's plan for my life. Our goals and dreams are unique to us. How does this purchase enhance the direction we are headed with life? Does it build into your lifestyle objectives and final goals? If so, then making the purchase may be wise. If not, it may not be optimal.

2. *Do I have inner peace about this expense?* Anxiety about a purchase is often a good indication that you should walk away from it. Good follow up questions might be, *"What will happen if I do not make this purchase?"* and *"How will it impact my life?"* Many times, our lives go on just fine without the things we think we need at the moment. A cup of coffee, ice cream at the Dairy Q, or a sale item at the clothing or grocery store may each be a small purchase, but together these small purchases add to a larger, more significant total amount. If you do not make unplanned purchases, you will avoid the pressure of trying to find the money you need to pay for them later when the bill becomes due.

3. For married couples, a third and very important question to ask is, *"Are my spouse and I in agreement?"* I have seen many couples in deep distress because one person made a purchase or series of purchases without consulting the other. If they had discussed the potential purchase, together they may have decided not make it or that it was a wise expenditure. The stress to the family because of a selfish or foolish decision is, in the long run, not worth the pleasure of the purchase.

If you ever believe your spouse would object or you find yourself reluctant to discuss a purchase with them, forego buying the item. A secret purchase will compromise the marriage relationship, and it is the marriage – not the item – that is of utmost importance. The value of the item will fade, but the marriage relationship will remain and should be given priority. Vote in favor of your marriage by walking away from the item. A healthy marriage is something that glorifies God and can provide sweet contentment. I have counseled numerous Christian couples that are on the verge of permanent separation because of the cumulative effect of small purchases that should have been avoided.

It Must Be Your Plan – Not Someone Else's

The Scriptures tell us to "*work out your salvation with fear and trembling . . . for his good pleasure*" (Philippians 2:12,13 NIV). The process of working out our salvation is the practical process of how we live the Christian life. Each day we encounter challenges, many of which are financial in nature. The financial decisions we make have both long- and short-term effects. The decision to purchase a piece of living-room furniture today will impact the ability to buy something else tomorrow and affect the total amount of debt we incur. Even the decision to spend $10.00 each day to purchase lunch instead of bringing lunch from home for $2.00 will influence how much money is available to spend on other things. This one decision about lunch represents an expense of $2,500 ($10 X 5 days X 50 work weeks = $2,500) this year on lunches instead of $500 ($2 X 5 days X 50 work weeks = $500). This additional $2,000 spent on purchasing lunch instead of bringing it from home is money not available for other things. The person who is $2,000 in debt with their credit card can have that debt removed in one year by simply designating the $8.00 that could be saved by bringing lunch each day toward paying off the credit card. The pressure of the money owed on the credit card will be gone and the person and their family will have less financial stress. This is a simple example of how living the Christian life wisely, through the "working out of your Salvation" with all seriousness, can impact a person's life. Foregoing immediate gratification so our life best reflects what we believe God intended is the "living out" of our salvation. It requires self-discipline.

Keep in mind that for most people, various points in life bring unique financial challenges. Sometimes people are dissatisfied with their lifestyle and feel like praying, "Lord, I don't think this is the right lifestyle for me right now. I need more money." Often it seems as if God responds with, "No, I need for you to have certain experiences today so you gain the depth of character that I desire for you. Though you may not understand it, I need for you to work through this experience right now. This is my plan for you." Typically, the way we gain character traits is when we experience difficult times. It has been said that we know the Lord loves us when He puts us through trying circumstances so we can build character and grow closer to Him. [James1: 2-12]

Working through the decision-making process about income and expenses is an opportunity for character growth. Some parents attempt to strongly influence how their adult children spend money. When this happens, tremendous relational tension can occur. Not only do the adult children find themselves frustrated with their parents, they also miss out on the opportunity to learn as they make financial decisions on their own. Together, married couples should learn to discuss their values, make decisions about both long- and short-term expenses, and live with the consequences. This process is an opportunity to grow in wisdom as they make decisions, some of which will be wise, and others possibly not.

I encourage those with whom I counsel to consider carefully Proverbs 1:5, which encourages the reader to listen to the advice of others and then to carefully make a decision. It does not compel the reader to accept the advice of others, but to consider it carefully. It is helpful to listen to the advice of our parents (Proverbs 23:22), who believe they are looking out for their adult children's best interests, and then to make our own decisions.

The spiritual journey is enhanced when we confidently make decisions and take actions after carefully considering information from a variety of sources. Remember, this process of making your own decisions and living with the consequences is what is meant by, "working out your salvation." Every decision impacts other areas of life. An expensive purchase today may make it difficult to buy other items in the future. It may also limit the opportunity to engage in certain activities because of the need to work more hours to pay off a purchase. It is because of the consequences of our decisions that we need to be careful and cautious, working out our salvation "with fear and trembling" when it comes to financial issues.

Wisdom comes to the person who learns how to make personal decisions about life, including financial decisions. Blindly following the instructions of a parent, pastor or advisor will not produce wisdom and spiritual maturity. Individuals and couples who learn how to make their own financial decisions will have the foundation necessary to make wise decisions in other areas in the future. This is a level of maturity and independence toward which they should strive.

Personality, Background, and Goals
Every person has a different personality, background, and set of goals, which influence the way they view life and make decisions. As a result they place varying emphasis on the quality of their home, its furnishings, the type of car driven, how much is put into savings and investments each month, the type of vacation taken, the amount of time designated to hobbies, how much is spent on gifts, how much is given to charities, how time is delegated to work, and the type of profession selected. These choices are not necessarily right or wrong; they are simply the preferences people possess. They in turn influence other decisions.

The family who highly values education will place emphasis there. Books and tuition will play a marked role. The family who values sports may spend money on athletic equipment, training, travel to games, and tickets to special events. The person who values leisure may choose an austere lifestyle so they can minimize the time they spend at work.

The family who takes the month of August to vacation at the same resort in the south of France each year will need to put away serious funds. To them, the impact of this annual gathering upon family unity may seem well worth the investment. The trip and the relationships and experiences it brings is something they truly value. Another family with the same income may feel that vacations are a waste of time. "After all," they may argue, "what tangible items does one gain from play? That time could instead be spent working to bring in income so the family can meet its financial obligations. A one-day trip to the beach each year is a sufficient break."

Differences in perspective can be significant. If a couple falls in love and determines to spend the rest of their lives together, only to learn that they each have very different perspectives on vacation, education, sports, or how much emphasis should be put on work in general versus leisure, they will need to spend serious time in conversation working out these differences. Most couples have many small and a few large differences. Learning to recognize these differences and make the necessary adjustments can be challenging.

In order to achieve family financial goals that blend priorities, it is important that each person learn the perspective of their partner. They need to sit, figuratively, in the chair of the other person and view the world from that person's perspective. By looking at the world from the perspective of the other person, they will be better able to understand what is important to that person. They can then work together as a couple to adjust their priorities so they can live in harmony. Candidness in conversations about priorities and the willingness to make adjustments to meet the needs of one another will greatly increase the richness of a marriage relationship.

The opportunity to make choices about where to spend money is good and can build character and draw a couple together. Many of those choices are not bad or good, or right or wrong. They are simply decisions that must be made. What is important, however, is the understanding that the result of these choices will influence other budgetary decisions. The judgments we make have to do with a number of influences, which include our personality, our background, and our goals.

Personality:
Some people seem by their very nature to be more conservative than others. They are slow to make decisions, spend as little money as possible, and may not enjoy change. Other people are spontaneous.

They buy items that are attractive to them, making instant decisions, sometimes without depth of thought. They tend to use credit cards freely, running high balances that never seem to be paid.

Most people tend to fall between these two spectrums. Personality is not something that absolutely determines whether we can manage money well, but it does influence behaviors and where money is spent.

Understanding if you and your spouse are by nature a **spender** who appreciates many things or a **saver** who desires future security will bring insight into how to best work together to develop an effective spending plan. Denial that such differences exist weakens the quality of your discussions together.

Background:
We are all influenced by our backgrounds, including our family and the things they valued while we were growing up:

- Did your family value long vacations as far from home as possible, or did they consider travel to be a waste of money and spend their vacation time relaxing at home?
- Did your family members spend a lot of money at Christmas, or was gift giving kept to a minimum?
- Did your family insist children begin working as soon as they were able, and did both parents spend sixty hours or more each week at work or did the family place very little value on work and therefore worked as few hours as possible?
- Was higher education a priority or were college expenses considered a waste?
- Was eating out a priority or did your family consider this to be a misuse of money?
- What was the house like in which you grew up? Did the cleanliness of the home matter and what emphasis was placed on its furnishings?

Family heritage and general environment in growing up play a part in the financial decisions we make now. Expectations that pertain to lifestyle are generally assumed. Recognizing this in our own life and in the life of our mate, allows us to consciously contemplate the influence they play on our values, goals and financial decisions. We can then adjust our values and expectations as needed to make the best decisions possible.

Goals:
Goals also influence how money is spent. The person who desires to be a missionary in an economically depressed neighborhood in Philadelphia or to poor rural communities in Oregon may need to concentrate on living a frugal life and paying off loans so they can move to their commission. The individual who sees herself in suburban America, living in a four-bedroom, 2-½-bath house, driving a van full of children, and enjoying social events at the country club will need to select the right kind of job, a given level of education, and invest money wisely. Personal goals will influence how money is spent in both the long and short term. The newlywed couples with whom I often counsel are sometimes surprised that their lifestyle expectations and goals are not congruent. I met with one couple in which the groom anticipated attending graduate school full-time for the next two years so he could become a poorly paid teacher in a small private school. The lady he desired to marry wanted to have children within the first year and to live in a wonderfully spacious home that would require a handsome income. The couple was experiencing conflict. Together, they addressed their goals and developed objectives that became a mutually compatible glue that has held them together. The process required many long conversations and the willingness to make significant sacrifices.

Personality, background, and personal goals each play a significant part in how we view personal finances. What financial plan is right? The answer is, "God made us each differently. His plan for each of us is unique. The way we spend our money will also be unique." There are, however, some principles we need to keep in mind so the decisions we make are wise. Among them is the need to recognize the impact these areas play on our financial and lifestyle choices.

The Little-Known Secret to Happiness in Life

While writing the book <u>Become the Person You're Meant To Be</u>, I learned what I consider to be the little-known secret to happiness in life. After much reading and hours of contemplation, it came to me. The secret to happiness in life, I determined, was *selflessness.* In looking at people who are very happy, I found they are usually the people who are outwardly focused. They are interested in other people, in listening to them, doing for them and making their lives more complete. Happiness seems to come to the person who *"selflessly gives of himself for the benefit of others."* Selfless people are those whom people gather around at parties because they are asking others to share ideas and thoughts about who they are and what is important to them. They are "other focused," not self-absorbed. Conversely, in observing people who are unhappy or depressed, we typically find individuals who are self-centered and looking out for their own personal needs before others. The focus of the attention of unhappy people is on what they want or believe they are entitled to, not on helping others.

As Christians, our focus should be on building up one another in love. Philippians 2:4 tells us, "Each of you should look not only to your own interests, but also to the interests of others" (NIV). When making financial decisions, the family member who thinks not just about personal desires, but considers carefully the desires of others, will by nature receive a dose of happiness. Now, I do not advocate being a complete pushover, allowing others to aggressively take advantage of your good intentions. I do, however, suggest that it is important to consider carefully the needs and desires of others when discussing financial issues and family goals.

The couple that is looking out for the best interests of each other will have a shift in their conversations about where to spend money.

Arguments will move from statements like, "No, honey, *I* want this." to, "No, honey, I want *you* to have those things." Selflessness comes in to play when a person thinks less about personal desires and more about what will best please their spouse. As a result, priorities shift and arguments dissipate. When there is unity in a marriage, and the couple works together, then the relationship is strengthened. Disagreements caused by selfishness tend to destroy a relationship. People who learn to look out for the best interests of their spouses are more likely to have a happy life because they're other-focused, and their marriage will be filled with peace and unity.

Priorities play a supreme role in personal finance. When making decisions, our relationship with God and the other people in our life that are important to us should be given high priority. Selflessness is the optimal word for building a sound financial future that responsibly manages the resources entrusted to us by God.

Discussion Questions and Assignments:

1. As you begin to implement the principles of personal finances in this book, set aside some time to speak with your spouse about financial issues each week. Indicate in the space provided the time and day you will meet. Day _____ Time ___:___. List the major areas you believe your conversation should cover during the first month.

    a. _____

    b. _____

    c. _____

    d. _____

2. The person who sets aside 15 minutes each week to focus specifically on paying bills and updating financial records should be able to keep financial records current. Some people are more gifted in organizing their time and records so the actual time spent will vary from person to person. Indicate the specific day and time you will dedicate specifically to this task.
    Day _____ Time ___:___ to ___:___.
    What are some of the obstacles you believe you will encounter as you strive to pay your bills and keep your financial records current?

3. It has been suggested that prayer can be helpful in determining appropriate lifestyle goals. Consider the prayer, *"Lord, let my will be your will."* How might this prayer create a difference in specific things or circumstances a person asks from the Lord and the goals the person sets for life?

4. Consider carefully Matthew 25:14-30.

    a. How does this parable influence the way you spend your money?

     b. How does this parable influence the goals you set for your life?

     c. How does this parable influence the kind of work you do for a living?

     d. How does this parable influence the number of hours you spend each week performing job related duties?

5. One of the most significant areas in which people struggle with their finances is how to know when a purchase is appropriate. Explain the three questions a person should ask when making a purchasing decision.

6. The Scriptures tell us to *"work out your salvation with fear and trembling"* (Philippians 2:12). What role does this verse play in making financial decisions?

7. Every person has a different personality, background, and set of goals. How does this influence your financial decisions? How might an understanding of this affect the way you discuss finances and make decisions with your spouse?

8. Proverbs 16:3 tells us to "Commit to the Lord whatever you do, and your plans will succeed." Provide guidelines for determining your financial plans for the future.

9. What is the little known *secret to happiness in life* as described in this chapter? Do you agree? Explain by giving examples to support your opinion.

10. Complete the Deed of Possessions as presented in this chapter. How does knowing that God owns everything you possess make a difference in how you will spend your time and money in the future?

Chapter 3: Establishing a Realistic Financial Plan

Knowing what we have and how much is being spent each month provides the insight needed to make wise financial decisions and establish control over personal finances. In my experience I have never met a couple with good financial records who are in financial trouble. Conversely, I have never met a couple in financial trouble that has more than a vague notion of how they are spending their money.

It is a basic business principle that companies with good financial records are more likely to succeed then companies with poor financial records. This does not mean that good financial records will guarantee a company's success. It does, however, mean that it is important for a business to have a good understanding of cash flow and its capital needs if it wants to succeed. After all, purchasing decisions, plans for expansion and even making payroll deadlines are based on an understanding of the availability and strength of resources.

In the same way, a family needs to have an understanding of the health of its financial condition. If a family wants to be free from debt and financial difficulties, its members need to have a good system of accountability for their money. Purchasing decisions require an understanding of when money will be available and the amount needed. The most practical tool for understanding and controlling family finances is a realistic, workable, budget or Personal Financial Plan. Called by some, the silver bullet for family financial success, the budget or Personal Financial Plan provides an understanding of and allows control over the decisions that need to be made.

When first learning about personal finance, I overheard an instructor ask a class of students for a good definition of a budget. To my surprise, the instructor gave a thought provoking response. His definition was just one word. The word was, "Freedom." Taken aback, I hardly objected. From my perspective, a budget provided anything but freedom. After all, it was a plan to restrict my free use of money. I saw it as a set of rules that would keep me from doing what I wanted to do with my funds, when I wanted, and the way I wanted. The big question was, " How does a budget provide freedom?"

The answer was as surprising as the definition. A realistic, workable budget or Family Financial Plan, he explained, will provide *freedom from worry*. People with a budget, will know at any given time if they are on track in reaching their financial objectives. They will know if the balance between income and spending is healthy and how much they have available to spend in various areas at any given time. A good financial plan removes the need to think about money all the time. Instead, a person is free to place their attention on living life and enjoying others.

It also provides the *freedom to make wise decisions*. When walking through a store and spying a desirable jacket, pair of shoes or home repair tool, we already know how much money is set aside for such purchases. As a result, we know if we can have the item now or if we need to wait until a later time. If a person does not have a financial plan, such decisions are based on guesswork. There is no knowledge of exactly how much money, if any, is available for such purchases, and of the impact the purchase will have financially.

A budget also provides *freedom of control*. Because we know how much money is available in various areas of the financial plan, we can make adjustments to spending that best meets our needs. The person who designates a given amount for the purchase of food during the week can decide how to best allocate these funds. If they spend a great deal for dinner today, they will do so knowing how much will be left for food at the end of the week. Spending the bulk of the food budget on steak or lobster today may create a need to have breakfast cereal or a box of macaroni and cheese for dinner later in the week. When a person knows how much is designated to a budgeted item, they are best able to control how this money is spent.

Freedom from worry, freedom to make wise decisions and freedom to control this aspect of life are three significant reasons for creating a budget and three powerful arguments for maintaining a budget. *Freedom from financial bondage* is a fourth benefit. When the pressure of personal finances seems out of control, people often feel as if they have a depressive black cloud hovering over their heads. This black cloud taints every aspect of their lives, including relationships with the people who are dearest to them. After all, those closest to them are often also victims of the lightening and drenching showers of depression produced by this dark cloud. The black cloud of financial bondage forces those under it to think constantly about money and feel the pressure it brings. Its impact can destroy a person's life spiritually, psychologically, and relationally. Couples often find this to be the source of daily altercations. A realistic, workable budget will bring *freedom* from this financial bondage by forcing a family to work together to establish priorities and identify a plan of action for getting control over their finances. It allows the freedom to spend money in areas they have identified together as most important to them. As a result, depression and irritability typically becomes a thing of the past. Couples have less reason to argue and a greater propensity to discuss together their goals and plans for the future. They are no longer pulled away from one another because of selfish spending and its related pressures. Instead, they are working together in support of mutual spending goals. Single men and women are better able to focus on the areas of their life that most interest them instead of feeling the pressure of poverty.

My wife, Kathy, posted some good advice on the bulletin board in our kitchen. She calligraphed the words, *"The most important things in life aren't things"* and posted it so we would see it every day. Her motivation was to help our family keep its priorities in check. So often, people spend the bulk of their time at work so they can have things, forgetting that the truly important things in life are relationships, not possessions.

This was confirmed a few years ago. While working as a nurse at Pennsylvania Hospital, where I cared mostly for older, cardiac patients, I decided to take a random poll of 20 patients who were over the age of 70. I asked them to think back over their lives and identify for me what they believed to be of most importance to them during their lifetime. The response was always the same. It was never the many opportunities they had to work overtime, their success in business, the car they drove, the size of their home or their role at church. In every case the answer was just one word. The word was "Family." Even patients who had never married or did not have children indicated that their extended family or a family they adopted over time was what mattered most.

Someday, as we reach the end of life, hopefully, we will have the chance to reflect on what has transpired over the years. Ideally, we will fondly remember the relationships we have nurtured with our family members, friends and our Lord. Logically, the things we desire to cherish at the end of life should be the things on which to focus when establishing financial goals and our budget. When designing our "freedom budget" or Personal Financial Plan, we need to constantly ask ourselves if the time with our employer and our family reflect an acceptable balance, and if the areas in which we spend our money enhance or detract from our true priorities. The famous seventeenth century theologian, Jeremy Taylor, summarized it well when he penned the words "The sublimity of wisdom is to do those things living which are to be desired when dying."

Setting Goals

Once priorities are affirmed, they help to shape goals, which in turn impact the budget and daily spending. For most people, goals are different during the various seasons of life. What is important to a person starting a career is much different from a person approaching retirement.

Typically, when a person first leaves their parents' home, they focus on their career and education and, once through college or established in their career, furnish their first home or apartment and spend money on social and sports events. Once married and they start a family, money is spent on diapers, baby furniture, children's clothing and related educational activities, sports and music lessons. As the middle years approach, future college costs can become a significant concern, and investing for retirement often becomes an issue. Even retirement comes in stages. During the first few years of retirement, a couple typically spends a great deal of money and energy doing things they have put off due to work and other obligations. Energy is spent on connecting with people and engaging in hobbies and travel. After the first seven years, a couple typically settles in to a more sedate lifestyle, requiring minimal financial drain. These seasons play out differently for each person, but the spending patterns and goals associated with each should be recognized. The corresponding need to adjust the budget should be made to meet these changing priorities.

Goals help draw a family together as they work toward common objectives. The GAP strategy is designed to provide a means of determining how to spend time and money in order to adopt an appropriate lifestyle. The GAP strategy is not simply about spending money, but is about making investments of time, effort, and priority in the future.

GAP Strategy

Goal
Analyze
Plan

The first step in implementing the GAP strategy is to establish **goals**. A healthy sequence of time intervals for these goals includes one year, five year and twenty year intervals. The person who lives in a small apartment in a not so nice economically depressed neighborhood, for example, may desire to live in a house in an upscale suburb. Someone working in a job that pays well, but is not in a field in which they have passion may determine they would like to have a change in career. Loren, a successful businessman in the Pacific Northwest, had reached the pinnacle of his career. Having started and built a printing company, he sold it to interested investors who, in turn, hired him to manage the enterprise. After several years of developing it further, he discussed with his wife his desire to become a psychologist. Calculating their finances and the time needed to invest in education and training, they worked together to make their dream a reality. Their commitment to an austere lifestyle while Loren attended school full-time, and their focus on reaching their mutually agreed upon objective, led to a much-desired change in career. A transformation in profession was desired and achieved because they were willing to write down the goals they needed to achieve in order to reach their objective. Individuals who desire a meaningful life need to take the time to reflect on what it is that they would like to achieve with their life. Is their current lifestyle what they want in the future? Does the profession or job they presently hold provide for them the level of satisfaction they desire? What are they providing for their family and friends that they would like to alter? Are they able to engage in the hobbies and leisure activities that are important to them? Do they spend the amount of time with their family that is desirable? What is it they would like to change in both the short and long term? One year, five year and twenty year goals set the stage for building a lifestyle that brings meaning and value.

Once lifestyle and financial goals are established, time should be set aside to ***analyze*** the current situation. What is the living environment like presently? What assets do we have by way of education and marketable skills? How much money has been saved or invested that might impact the future? Is debt an obstacle to future plans? Can goals be met by continuing on the current life course, or are changes necessary? A person who lives in the ghetto and works a part-time job at minimum wage is not likely to earn enough money throughout his lifetime to live in an upscale suburban neighborhood. A professional, such as a doctor, salesman or lawyer, will never pay off outstanding debt if more is spent than earned. Analyzing current circumstances and identifying obstacles and assets is a necessary step in bringing goals to fruition.

The final step is to develop a *plan* for getting from where a person is today to where they would like to be in the future. It may be that more education or training to acquire a marketable skill is necessary to achieve a higher paying job. A specific plan to pay off debt may allow a couple to live a more leisurely, stress free life. Retirement may seem like an unattainable dream, but by setting a specific plan that will impact how money is spent and saved, it will be possible. Setting goals, analyzing our current situation and setting a plan in action will only be effective if bathed in prayer. Plans should be as detailed as possible, and self-discipline of the highest level may be required to implement the plan of action, but follow through with a daily request to God for His blessing will help bring the plan to reality.

Designing a Personal Financial Plan

Once priorities are examined and goals established, the foundation is laid to prepare a realistic, workable budget. A budget geared toward a lifestyle or set of goals to which you are not committed will not work. Frankly, a budget will only work if those who must live with the budget believe it meets their personal objectives. The married couple that establishes a budget that is out of balance for one person, demanding sacrifice from them and favors the other will find it to be ineffective. The single person who establishes a budget that fits a lifestyle to which they cannot adapt will be unable to be compliant with the guidelines they have set. We must determine what is really important in life and design a budget that reflects these values. Provided below are the four Ds of designing a realistic, workable budget.

Designate a time to complete the budget or Personal Financial Plan. It is important to designate a specific target date by which to have it completed. With an end date in mind, the completion is measurable by both time and by action. That is, you will know what is to be done and when it should be completed. Typically, a budget will involve a number of drafts. "First draft" means that all the spaces are filled in, but numbers are not permanent. Later drafts will reflect adjustments that become apparent after careful thought and reflection have taken place.

Discuss the budget as a couple or family. Once you set a deadline, set aside specific times to discuss and begin working on the budget so you can meet your deadline. If you plan to do the budget within the next to weeks, for example, schedule at least an hour each week to sit down and talk through it together. Go through the numbers and see what makes sense to you. You need to discuss it as a couple, and possibly as a family, because the budget impacts everyone.

Determine to be committed to the Personal Financial Plan. Once you put the plan together, it is up to you to make it work. It will not be effective if numbers are drafted, only to be ignored. Each person who spends money in the family budget must be held accountable for adherence.

Decide to keep it current. Remember that life is a journey. As such, unexpected events will emerge during your travels. It is therefore necessary to make adjustments along the way. Once your Financial Plan is established there will be unexpected expenses, windfalls, and circumstances.

Resolving Differences

Families often experience differences in how individual members believe money should be allocated. The thirteen-year-old athlete believes life centers around soccer and basketball. Personalized lessons that help him excel to his greatest potential are, in his mind, a must. His mom believes a safe and reliable automobile should be expected and she is willing to spend whatever it takes to keep her family safe while traveling. His dad loves to spend money on a weekly round of golf. This time of relaxation with his friends is important to him and sets the tone for the rest of his week. With limited resources, it may be that when priorities are finalized, not everyone will be able to experience their expectations. The result may be disappointment, anger, resentment and intense arguments. When families disagree, there are several principles that can be used to ease the transition between expectations and reality.

First, when formulating a personal financial plan, listen carefully to one another.

Next, *listen to one other.* Allow each party to express a desire and explanation of his or her rationale for an expenditure without passing judgment. The husband might say, for example, "I believe we should put money toward a boat. Having a boat would bring us together as a family." The wife's role at this point is to listen without interrupting, allowing her husband to give a full explanation. After he has had an opportunity to share his feelings she can then respond with her rationale as to why this expenditure should be avoided or altered at this time.

Typically, it is not necessary for a decision to be made immediately. While the pressure may be felt to finalize the family budget, resolving an issue instantly may not bring optimal results. Allowing some time to contemplate issues that are not easily resolved is time well spent. Experience teaches that the stew that sits on the back burner of the stove simmering all day is the stew that has the deepest savor. In the same way, decisions that are allowed to sit without resolution for a while are often richer in value. After listening to one another, time should be allocated for each side to consider the issue. This allows everyone to think about the information and desires presented by others and to think about alternatives that might not be considered if a decision were made in the heat of the moment. A well-oiled budget is not drafted in one sitting. Some issues are better decided after taking time to think about them and consider alternatives. The desire to save money for a down payment so the family can move to a different neighborhood, or send their children to a private school, or purchase a boat, or take individualized soccer or basketball lessons may take on a different nature after time has been taken to think through the ramifications and the impact it has on others.

This leads us to the three keys to building an effective family budget. The first is for each member to be willing to *compromise* with one another. The second is for each member to think beyond their personal needs and be willing to *compromise* with one another. And yes, you have guessed it – the third is to have the willingness to *compromise* for the good of the family and relationships at large. Unfortunately, the thrust of thinking for many people is to think of them putting self first. They selfishly believe they are more important than others and are therefore entitled to special privileges. This is contrary to what is needed to build a healthy family. The essential ingredient for any family's health is for members to give of themselves for the welfare of others by listening to them and looking to fulfill what is best for them.

Determining Personal Financial Plan Allocations

There is a natural process for determining the actual amount to allocate to various aspects of the budget. First, write in the numbers on your budget worksheet that do not change from month to month. You know for example that your tithe will be 10% of your income. You also know the amount of your monthly mortgage or rent payment, what your income and property taxes will be, your life insurance premiums, automobile payments, retirement savings and other fixed costs.

Once these numbers are established, the second area to explore is items that may vary from month to month. Determining these numbers will be based on your *past experience*. There are several tools that can be used to help determine these numbers. One that is very helpful is the *"Overview of Expenses"* form presented in the appendix of this chapter. This tool allows the user to review the amount of money spent in a given area each month. It reveals trends and the actual amount that needs to be allocated. The amount of money spent on the targeted budget item can be observed in a person's checkbook or bank statement for each month during the past year. Knowing the average amount allows for money to be put away during months when expenses will be low so they will be available when expenses are high. For example, typically heating bills are higher in January and February than they are in May and June and expenses for air conditioning are higher in August than in March; expenses for gifts rise drastically in December. Noting these trends, the average amount spent can be prorated and money kept aside in reserve during months in which expenses are low so they are available when expenses are high. Maintaining this reserve will ease tension during those months in which expenses are high. It will, however, require self-discipline. After all, the money on reserve in the bank for future expenses can be a temptation when the desire to purchase something emerges. But knowing the money is available to cover upcoming needs, and the corresponding peace of mind it brings, will be well worth the discipline.

There are several expenses that are known for sneaking up in a budget, sometimes with disastrous results. The most notable of these is Christmas. Planning ahead for this event is important. How unfortunate is the family who purchases wonderful gifts for one another only to be dismayed when the bill comes in January. Learning they are more deeply in debt than they imagined, it may take the rest of the year to pay off their extravaganza. Putting $50 away each month for Christmas, and spending only the $600 saved for this celebration, frees the family from the chains of financial bondage that over indulgence can bring.

This same principle holds true for vacations. Many families fail to plan and save for their vacation, simply placing the expenses on their credit card. The resulting bill, when added to their other outstanding obligations, can be overwhelming. Creating a set amount for vacation, and systematically saving for the event each month, allows a family to have the funds available at the time of their vacation.

Identifying expenses and placing them on the "Overview of Expenses" form provides the information needed to create an accurate budget. Actual expenses are available and will form the base on which to make decisions for the future. Knowing the family historically spends $600 a year on gifts allows them to determine how much they wish to spend to add or remove from next year's budget based on other financial needs.

The *experience of others* builds on known expenses and past experiences. Listening to the insights of family and friends, searching the internet, attending seminars and reading books like the one you hold in your hand can provide helpful insights. This is especially true for newly married couples or when purchases are made that are out of the ordinary. When considering the installation of an in ground swimming pool, a family will be well advised to talk with several vendors, friends and acquaintances to learn the hidden costs and avoid costly mistakes.

Recommended Budget Allocations
The question is often asked, "How much do the experts say we should put into the various categories of our Personal Financial Plan?" Fortunately, there are many books and websites that provide this information. The amounts listed at the end of this chapter are based on a culmination of insights from these experts. A family should use these numbers as guidelines to see if they are on target. The overarching principle is that expenses cannot exceed income. A family may decide to spend more on housing than is recommended. In doing so, they will need to reduce the amount spent on some other areas to compensate for exceeding the recommended amount to be spent on their home. It is all about balance and staying within spending boundaries.

A realistic, workable, budget is the silver bullet for establishing and maintaining financial sanity. It takes work and will only be effective if the family is committed to it and establishes the discipline needed to live by the standards to which they have agreed.

Discussion Questions and Assignments:

1. Consider the definition given for a budget. Do you agree with the premise that the word Freedom accurately defines a budget? Explain.

2. Explain the impact a realistic, workable financial plan will have on worry, decision making and control over various areas of life.

3. What is financial bondage? How does this impair a person's feelings, interaction with other members of the family and spiritual life?

4. Reflect on the sayings "the most important things in life aren't things" and the words by Jeremy Taylor, "The sublimity of wisdom is to do those things living which are to be desired when dying." How does this impact the financial goals you set for yourself and your family both in the short term and in the future?

5. Consider the acronyms GAP as described above. How comfortable are you with setting goals and establishing action plans to see these goals become a reality? What obstacles hold you back from establishing realistic obtainable goals and seeing those goals become reality?

6. Describe the four Ds for establishing a personal financial plan. Why is each step important?

7. What are some steps a family can take to resolve disagreements about how much should be allocated to various portions of the budget?

8. Establish a Personal Financial Plan or budget for your personal finances. Complete each section adjusting the numbers to meet your personal lifestyle. Adjust the budget so that the amount you spend each month does not exceed your income. Use the

"Overview of Expenses" to calculate accurate numbers for each line.

9. Identify the rules for establishing a sound budget. Explain why each is important.

10. Identify the challenges you experience as you draft your first Personal Financial Plan. Discuss these with a friend and identify below the advice they shared.

11. A Personal Financial Plan is not optional. It is the center-piece or silver bullet of a healthy budget. Why is this?

12. Describe steps you can take to adjust your Personal Financial Plan so it remains relevant to your financial needs in the years ahead.

Percentage Guide of Family Income

Gross Income	Up to $17,000	$69,000	$139,000	$212,300	$379,151 or more
Tithe of Gross	10%	10%	10%	10%	10%
State Tax*	2%	3%	3%	4%	5%
Federal Tax**	10%	15%	25%	28%	33%
Spendable Income	**$13,360**	**$50,925**	**$89,083**	**$129,487**	**$212,581**
Savings	5%	5%	5%	5%	5%
Transportation	12%	15%	13%	12%	11%
Food	15%	12%	9%	7%	6%
Insurance	8%	7%	4%	4%	4%
Entertainment/ Recreation	2%	2%	2%	2%	2%
Clothing	5%	5%	6%	6%	6%
Medical/Dental	5%	4%	4%	3%	3%
Misc.	5%	3%	5%	5%	5%
Housing	38%	37%	36%	35%	33%
Debt Reduction	5%	5%	5%	5%	5%
Investments		5%	9%	13%	15%

*Varies by state
**Adjusted annually by the internal Revenue Service

Overview of Expenses

Overview of Expenses	Monthly Budget	January	February	March	April	May	June	July	August	September	October	November	December
INCOME													
Salary One													
Salary Two													
Interest													
Dividends													
Other ( )													
Other ( )													
Total Net Income													
EXPENSES													
Tithe (of gross)													
Mission #1													
Mission #2													
Other #1													
Other #2													
Total													
SAVINGS													
401K/403B #1													
401K/403B #2													
Emergency Fund													
Other Funds													
Christmas/Bday													
Car Replacement													
Total													
HOUSING													
Insurance													
Property Taxes													
Electricity													
Gas/Oil													
Water/Sewer													
Trash Removal													
Regular Maintenance													
Scheduled Repairs													
Pool Maintenance													
Lawn Care													
Alarm Service													
Other ( )													
Other ( )													
Total													

Overview of Expenses

Overview of Expenses	Monthly Budget	January	February	March	April	May	June	July	August	September	October	November	December
FOOD													
Groceries													
Coffee/Lunch													
Fast Food													
Total													
CLOTHING													
Children													
Adults (Personal)													
Work Related													
Other ( )													
Total													
Transportation													
Bus/Train													
Car Payment #1													
Car Payment #2													
Gas													
Tolls													
Scheduled Maintenance													
Repairs													
License/Tags													
Insurance													
Total													
INSURANCE													
Life													
Medical													
Dental													
Other ( )													
Total													
MEDICAL EXPENSES													
Physician													
Dentist													
Optometrist													
Prescription													
Other ( )													
Total													
DEBTS													
Credit Card #1													
Credit Card #2													
Credit Card #3													
Credit Card #4													
Loan #1													
Loan #2													
Loan #3													
Loan #4													
Other ( )													
Other ( )													
Total													

Overview of Expenses

Overview of Expenses	Monthly Budget	January	February	March	April	May	June	July	August	September	October	November	December
Entertainment/ Recreation													
Vacation													
Special Trips													
Baby-Sitter													
Dining Out													
Other (___)													
Other (___)													
Total													
Miscellaneous													
Toiletry & Cosmetics													
Beauty Shop & Barber													
Laundry/Cleaners													
Subscriptions													
Education													
Cash (Husband)													
Cash (Wife)													
Cable/Internet													
Telephone													
Household Items													
Other (___)													
Other (___)													
Other (___)													
Total													

Personal Financial Plan
Monthly Income and Expenses

INCOME PER MONTH		TAXES & FICA	
Salary One	_____	Federal Income Tax	_____
Salary Two	_____	State Income Tax	_____
Interest	_____	City Wage Tax	_____
Dividends	_____	St Unemployment Tax	_____
		FICA Social Sec	_____
Other (_____)	_____	FICA Medicare	_____
Other (_____)	_____	Pretax Medical	_____
Other (_____)	_____	Pretax Dental	_____
TOTAL:	_____	**TOTAL:**	_____

EXPENSES:
TITHE (of gross)

Local Church	_____	Spendable Income #1.	_____
Mission #1 ( )	_____	Spendable Income #2.	_____
Mission #2 ( )	_____	**TOTAL:**	_____
Other #1 ( )	_____		
Other #2 ( )	_____		
TOTAL:	_____		

Personal Financial Plan
Monthly Income and Expenses

1. SAVINGS

401K/4Q3B #1 _____

401K/4Q3B #2 _____

Auto Withdrawal _____

Emergency Fund _____

Other Funds _____

Christmas/B-days _____

Car Replacement _____

TOTAL: _____

2. HOUSING

Mortgage/Rent _____

Insurance _____

Property Taxes _____

Electricity _____

Gas/Oil _____

Water/Sewer _____

Trash Removal _____

Equipment/Tools _____

Regular Maintenance _____

Scheduled Repairs _____

Pool Maintenance _____

Lawn Care _____

Alarm Service _____

Other (___) _____

Other (___) _____

TOTAL: _____

3. FOOD

Groceries _____

Coffee/Lunch _____

Fast Food _____

Other _____

TOTAL: _____

4. CLOTHING

Children _____

Adults (Personal) _____

Work Related _____

Other ( ) _____

TOTAL: _____

5. TRANSPORTATION

Bus/Train _____

Car Payment #1 _____

Car Payment #2 _____

Gas/Tolls _____

Scheduled

Maintenance _____

Repairs _____

License/Tags

(reserve) _____

Insurance _____

Other _____

TOTAL: _____

Personal Financial Plan
Monthly Income and Expenses

6. INSURANCE

Life _____
Medical _____
Dental _____
Other ( ) _____
TOTAL: _____

7. MEDICAL EXPENSES

Physician _____
Dentist _____
Optometrist _____
Prescriptions _____
Other ( )
Other ( ) _____
TOTAL: _____

8. DEBTS

Credit Card #1 _____
Credit Card #2 _____
Credit Card #3 _____
Credit Card #4 _____
Loan #1 _____
Loan #2 _____
Loan #3 _____
Other ( ) _____
Other ( ) _____
TOTAL: _____

9. ENTERTAINMENT/ RECREATION

Vacation _____
Special Trips _____
Baby-sitter _____
Dinning Out _____
Other ( ) _____
Other ( ) _____
TOTAL: _____

10. MISCELLANEOUS

Toiletry/Cosmetics _____
Beauty Shop/Barber _____
Laundry/Cleaning _____
Subscriptions _____
Education _____
Cash (Husband) _____
Cash (Wife) _____
Cable/Internet _____
Phone _____
Household Items _____
Other ( ) _____
Other ( ) _____
Other ( ) _____
TOTAL: _____
INCOME STATEMENT
Total Spendable Income
Total Expenses _____
Difference _____

Chapter 4: Living with Your Financial Plan

"Do you know how to make God laugh?" my nephew, R.J., asked as we walked to the parking lot.

"I must admit, I don't know," was my response.

"Just tell Him what you think you are going to do tomorrow," he replied.

I just smiled. R.J. was so right. We make all kinds of plans and think we know our immediate and long-term future – but only God knows what is really going to happen. In James 4:13-15 the Bible says, *"Now listen, you who say, 'Today or tomorrow we will go to this or that city, spend a year there, carry on business and make money.' Why, you do not even know what will happen tomorrow. What is your life? You are a mist that appears for a little while and then vanishes. Instead, you ought to say, 'If it is the Lord's will, we will live and do this or that."*
Yes, the future is a mystery.

My conversation with R.J. led me to consider the ramifications of our uncertain futures on the family budget. Sure, it is both a mature and responsible behavior to establish a family budget. Planning for the future is something we find the Apostle Paul doing, as well as Daniel, King David, and King Saul. Getting a handle on anticipated events is what a family budget is all about. It is the process of identifying the amount of money we expect to have available during the month or year and then determining where we believe it should be spent. But much of the future is and always will be a mystery. We plan the best we can and hopefully are able to adjust the budget along the way. Unfortunately for some couples, once they agree on a budget, their commitment is immutable, and they refuse to make any adjustments to their numbers. They believe the amounts they have designated are solid and based upon a realistic understanding of their financial situation. They will not, therefore, adjust these numbers, regardless of the circumstances. If they allow flux, they believe it means they are violating the commitment they have made in good faith to their future.

It is true that a commitment to maintaining a budget gives the budget credibility and value, but refusing to adjust the budget along the way removes the ability to adapt to changes. Typically, a budget, when first established, is about 80% accurate. There are many small things we fail to consider because of unknown factors. Initially, the budget should be tested over several months and adapted as needed before confidence in its accuracy is established. Even then, minor adjustments may need to be made to reflect lifestyle changes and unforeseen circumstances. As the saying goes, "People make plans, and then life happens."

A realistic, workable, written budget is at the heart of getting our finances in order and remaining free from financial bondage. A budget takes discipline and work, but it is part of the process of moving from a troubled situation to a place where people have control over their finances. It is not uncommon for families to go through the exercise of creating a budget only to give up on it after a month or two because it was unrealistic. The process of drafting a budget is a futile exercise if it is not a helpful tool. It needs to be an instrument that functions effectively and adjusts to change.

Safeguards To Ensure a Sound Budget

Establishing accurate numbers when establishing a budget is an art. There are several safeguards that can be taken to ensure the budget is sound.

1. **Budget on the High Side**
A broad rule of thumb for determining budgetary numbers is to always designate a little more money than you think is necessary. This provides a natural cushion that compensates for those areas in which the estimation is unexpectedly low. My friend Anne and her husband Duane moved from a home that was a small one-story rancher to a two-story house. The new house being two stories instead of one was more than double the size of the old. As a result, they expected their heating bill to be twice as high. What they learned was that the cost of

heating their home was far less than they had budgeted. The new big house actually cost less to heat using gas than their small house with its electric baseboard heaters. That was the good news. The bad news was that they expected their taxes to be close to what the realtor had told them. To their surprise they were actually twice that amount. Fortunately, because they had budgeted on the high side for heating and several other areas, they were able to accommodate the unexpected expense.

It is also easy to give ourselves the benefit of the doubt when budgeting. Couples frequently write in a low amount for the heating bill, reasoning they are going to keep the temperature at 66 degrees and wear sweaters when the weather turns cold. But when winter comes and the discomfort of the chilly air becomes too great, the thermostat is generally turned up and consequently the heating bill increases. Budgeting on the high side provides a buffer that is especially necessary when forming the first draft with numbers that have not been established over time. The numbers then tend to be slanted toward a higher tendency of accuracy. Remember, the goal is to establish a budget with realistic numbers, and budgeting on the high side provides just that.

2. Know Where the Money Will Come From
Before making any purchase or establishing a budget, it is essential to determine where the money will come from. Working in the business world, my friend Kevin sometimes gets occasional bonuses. Knowing in advance the approximate amount of the anticipated bonus, he thinks about a variety of ways in which the money could be spent. Sharing his dreams with his wife, a very practical lady, she frequently reminds him that the money is not yet in his hand. Her caution is to not make plans to make expenditures until the check is actually cashed. After all, any number of things can happen to reduce or eradicate the amount.

I have counseled people who have told me, "I know I'm operating in a financial deficit right now, but that's okay because, I'm . . . expecting an inheritance/receiving a settlement from a law suit / anticipating an income tax refund . . . and when I get that money, then I will be able to pay my financial obligations." My response to them is always the same, "When you actually have the money in your possession you will be able to spend it. Until then, it is just wishful thinking. Make your future plans based on actual income." Dreams are wonderful and spur hope for the future. When budgeting, however, they can bring expectations that are too optimistic, an unrealistic budget and ultimately disappointment.

3. Income Must Equal Expenses
It may be possible for the government to spend more than it receives in income. After all, it prints the money. However, since it is against the law for us to print money, we can't deficit spend indefinitely. Our only option is to spend less money than we bring in. If we find we are spending more money than we budgeted, then we must make adjustments in our budget, and live with those adjustments. Yes, it may mean we must make some serious changes, even changes in life style that we do not like, but we cannot spend more than we make without dire consequences.

4. Live Within Your Budget
It is not uncommon for a family to have a mortgage or payments on a boat, car or vacation house that leaves them without the resources they need to meet their other obligations. This situation is called being "house (boat, car, vacation) poor." The result is tension due to not having sufficient funds for other desires and necessities like recreation, clothes, food, medical care, automobiles and other things. Maude and Larry were able to put 5% down on a new home due to the generous lending guidelines established by the FHA. Their mortgage exceeded 40% of their income but, it was a beautiful house and exceeded anything Maude had every dreamed of. She was willing to cut back on everything else in order to move into this fabulous building. Eighteen months later, Maude came to me in deep distress. Her dream home was destroying their family harmony. It was difficult to forego doing the things they did before they moved into the house. There were no more bowling nights for Maude, Saturday golf for Larry, soccer

lessons for their children, and even keeping up with their regular bills became difficult. After much discussion, it became apparent that they needed to make the difficult choice to sell their domicile and move to a home that would allow for a better balance. For Maude and Larry, the decision to sell their home was extremely hard, but the result of reducing the large expense of their mortgage in order to free funds for a life with a healthy balance was worth the change. Harmony and financial stability have returned.

5. Continually Revise the Budget

Finally, financial circumstances continually change. As a family moves through the various seasons of life, needs and desires change. Young children stop using diapers and baby formula and begin attending soccer practice, taking piano lessons and dressing for school. A van or crossover instead of the small two-door economy car may become a necessity. The budget that is flexible will allow for change, making it a practical tool that adjusts to a family's ever changing needs.

The Monthly Budget Review, which is provided below, is a tool designed to analyze spending patterns so the budget can be adjusted appropriately. On this form. the amount spent in the major areas of the budget are recorded in the first column. In the next column the user writes in the actual expense. The third column is used to calculate the difference, if any, between these two. If the difference is significant, comments explaining this can be written in the fourth column. If, for example, $800 was budgeted for food in December, yet $1,200 was actually spent, the family needs to evaluate the cause for the difference. If the difference is due to the massive number of relatives that came to visit for the celebratory season of Christmas, the extra expense represents a one-time situation. Christmas will not reappear for another year and therefore the budget will not need to be adjusted. However, if the food budget is consistently over budget by $400 due to real costs, an adjustment in the amount designated for this area is necessary.

Most people need to use the Monthly Budget Review form when they are in the process of creating their first budget. The first three to four months are critical for establishing an accurate account of how money is spent. Then, after they have determined a realistic allotment for each category, they need only to reevaluate the budget using this form annually or semi-annually. Expenses tend to migrate, morph, and mutate. The Monthly Budget Review evaluates the need to adjust spending so the budget reflects reality and ultimately a healthy lifestyle. Remember, a budget is a plan to control the flow of money. It is not a law. It is a tool designed to work for you and should allow for the flexibility that contributes to changes in life.

Monthly Financial Plan Review

Expense Item	Current Budget	Actual Expense	Difference	Comments	Adjusted Budget
Tithe					
Savings					
Housing					
Food					
Clothing					
Transportation					
Insurance					
Medical Expenses					
Debt Reduction					
Entertainment & Recreation					
Miscellaneous					
TOTAL					

Managing a family's financial plan effectively requires the implementation of several essential guidelines.

1. One Person Should be in Charge of Each Bill

The first of these guidelines is that *one person should be in charge of each bill*. Every bill that comes into the home must have an owner. If no one "owns" a bill and is ultimately responsible to see that it is paid, it is easy for the bill to remain outstanding long after it is due. Who is assigned to each bill will be different for each family. In some homes, one person is responsible to pay all of the bills. In others, bills may be divided based on an individual's activities or interests. In one home the wife may be in charge of paying for the groceries because she is the one who does most of the cooking. The husband may be responsible for lawn care, cars, and home repair because these are his areas of responsibility. By dividing bill payments based on interests and areas of responsibility, a bill can be delegated to the appropriate person. In turn, amounts allocated in the budget to each person must reflect the money needed to pay the bills that will come due.

2. Both Parties Should Know How to Manage the Finances

Regardless of who makes payments, *both parties should know how to pay the bills*. After all, what will happen if the person who pays the bills becomes incapacitated or dies unexpectedly? Ralph and Alisha had what they considered the perfect arrangement. Ralph worked in construction during the week and Alisha stayed at home, managing their household, including all of the finances. Over the course of time Alisha contracted breast cancer and ultimately passed away. This was a difficult time for Ralph as he went through the bereavement process and adjusted to his life without her. One of the more difficult changes was learning how she had managed the family finances. He was clueless about anything related to this aspect of their marriage. He did not know if she had life insurance, which bank they used, where the checkbook was kept, how much they had in savings, or even how to deposit funds into their checking account. As a result, this time of bereavement was also a financial nightmare. Fortunately, his sister-in-law Barbara also controlled the money in her household and was able to step in and help Ralph. Together they spent many hours sorting through files and electronic documents until, over time, they were able to determine where various documents were and set up a system for paying and tracking expenses that worked for him. How nice it would have been if Alisha and Ralph had discussed the financial aspect of their family with one another regularly so that they both knew the nuances of how their money was handled.

3. Decide on the Number of Checking Accounts Needed
One question couples need to address is the number of checking accounts. Some families believe that because they love each other and desire to share everything they should also share their checkbook. This is practical if one person is responsible for paying most of the bills. Others, because each person is in charge of separate bills or have a different style of recordkeeping decide they should each manage checking accounts separately. From a purely pragmatic perspective, the person who is very detail oriented and figures their records to the very penny, will become frustrated with a partner who rounds off checks to the nearest dollar or is less demanding when it comes to keeping track of expenditures. If balancing the checkbook due to different styles causes conflict, the couple should discuss their options, including separate checking accounts. The goal is to design and use a system that works effectively and builds the relationship.

Those who choose separate checking accounts should establish joint ownership of each account. If trouble occurs such as illness or death, the accessibility to funds and the ability to manage them will be easy. Complete transparency builds trust. Both parties should be able to go online or otherwise view all financial statements. This will allow them to see how money is managed and the amount available at any time and add to the knowledge needed when making financial decisions. Openness in this, as well as all aspects of marriage, provides a better relationship. Secret accounts or cash hidden behind a picture fit within this same rule. They should not be a part of any marriage. The openness that is important to a healthy marriage is violated when secrets raise their ugly faces.

The Envelope Method

My favorite style of managing family finances is the primitive but effective "Envelope Method." Nearly all financial experts who counsel people wanting to get out of debt recommend this method when appropriate. Essentially, it is a physical, hands-on, pre-allocation of money. Very practical and easy to implement, an envelope is designated for each category of the budget. The envelope is labeled with the category it represents. Money placed in an envelope to be used to purchase food will be labeled as "food." The envelope containing money for recreation will be labeled as "recreation." The money used to purchase clothing will be labeled as "clothing." At the beginning of each month, the money designated for a specific area is placed into an envelope. When funds are needed the money is extracted and used for that purpose. If $100 is designated for food, the person purchasing food will go to the envelope and withdraw the necessary funds from that envelope and use it to pay for food. As the money dwindles in size everyone knows how much is left and they can manage spending to reflect available resources. If the money runs out before the end of the month, it is a signal that either not enough money was budgeted for that category, or they have overspent. Putting receipts and paid invoices in the envelope from which money has been taken or writing specific purchases and the dates of such on the outside of the envelope, makes it easy to review expenses and decide if adjustments need to be made to the budget or if spending patterns need to be altered.

The envelope method can be used for every area of the budget or for selective categories. Brian Giggs likes to work on his yard. For a long time he had an envelope with money designated for yard improvement. Throughout the year, Brian would add cash to the envelope, notably money that came as gifts or if he had something extra at the end of the month. When the season for yard work came, he knew exactly how much money he could spend on shrubs, rocks, dirt, pavers and construction material. Brian found the envelope method provided an effective means of rationing money for various aspects of the budget so that overspending could be eliminated.

Some people complain that the envelope method requires using "cash only" and is, therefore, inconvenient and that credit card purchases make it less painful than parting with cash. That is the point. The intent of the exercise is to reduce spending to the amount designated in the budget and no more.

Debit cards are convenient and they have a quality that is useful in curbing spending. While a credit card allows the user to borrow money from the bank to make purchases, the debit card restricts the amount that can be spent to the sum that is in the user's checking account. Once the money in the checking account is depleted, purchases can no longer be made. When Brian arrives at the hardware store to purchase paint and supplies, his debit card takes money directly from his checking account to make the payment. If he uses all of the money available in his checking account, his temptation to purchase additional supplies is curbed because his resources have been depleted. He needs only to replenish his account to again use his debit card for budgeted purchases.

A budget or financial plan that includes where money will come from and where it will be spent is essential for financial health. This plan is a tool you design to fit the needs of your family. As such, a budget or financial plan is a tool each family should design to fit their particular situation. It will, of course, only be effective if it is respected and adhered to. Making excuses for not sticking to a budget is not acceptable. A family needs to understand the principles behind the budget and agree to the decisions that lead to the allocations made for each expenditure.

Discussion Questions and Assignments:

1. Commitment to adhere to a budget is important. After all, a financial plan is of little value if it is not followed. Under which circumstances might a budget be adjusted?

2. Why is it important to budget numbers in a financial plan that are slightly higher than expected? Give an example.

3. "It is a sure thing," exclaims Stephanie. "I am going to get the raise in salary. All I have to do is to get a promotion and that will happen next month. Let's go ahead and sign the lease agreement for the new apartment now." What warning would you give Stephanie to protect her from financial trauma?

4. Describe how the Monthly Budget Review works. Use it for a month and record the differences it identified between anticipated expenses and reality.

5. "We just leave the bills on the desk and then when someone has the time, they pay them." What are the disadvantages of this method? Why is it important that "one person be the owner of each bill?"

6. Some families have one person who loves to pay all of the bills. Why is it important that both the husband and wife know the nuances of how their money is handled?

7. What are the advantages of having one checkbook from which the family pays its bills? What are the advantages of having more than one checkbook? Which is most practical for you?

8. Why is financial transparency important to a marriage?

9. Describe the "Envelope Method" of budgeting. Explain the advantages and disadvantages of this approach.

10. Explain the advantages of using a debit card over a credit card? What are the advantages of using a credit card over a debit card?

11. What challenges did you find in formulating your budget or Financial Plan? How did you overcome them?

12. Did you find the Overview of Expenses helpful in creating your budget? Explain.

Chapter 5: Making Wise Allocations in Your Financial Plan

Facing the blank page of a Personal Financial Plan Worksheet may seem overwhelming. Where do you start with allocating your income into the expense categories? The pages ahead offer insight and money-saving tips to help you determine how much to designate for housing, food, clothing, transportation, insurance, and entertainment, as well insights for deciding your income level.

Income: What are you trying to accomplish?
The first item in the Personal Financial Plan Worksheet is income. My friend Pierce, who used to be the vice president of a bank, spent the bulk of his time visiting very wealthy people. He often went to their homes to help them with their investments. On one memorable occasion, he and one of his colleagues went to the home of a family that was particularly well off. They drove along the driveway only to spy a tennis court on one side of the drive, a swimming pool on the other side, and stables in the back of the house. It was a palatial home with immaculate landscaping, fine rugs, art and statues, exquisite furniture and domestic help. They went in to meet with the people only to find them to be notably unhappy. The couple had a splintered marriage (the husband's third) due to the stress, selfish attitude and investment of time associated with the way the family had acquired wealth. The children loved their possessions, but displayed visible hatred for their parents. Bitterness and suspicion permeated their conversation.

This visit was not unusual for Pierce and his associate. Many of the people with whom he worked were unhappy, but wealthy. This visit was, however, an iconic example he used to describe people who failed to build a family, and had instead built an empire. It sparked conversation about what Pierce and his colleague saw in the lives of many of their clients. Together they set the objective not to let this happen to them. They desired to have nice things, but not at the expense of losing the love and camaraderie their families possessed.

It's not just wealthy people who live this way. Your neighbors may not have tennis courts, swimming pools, or stables, but they might be working long hours pursuing "the American dream," only to find they have lost the pleasure of a meaningful family life. The question to ask ourselves is, "what are we trying to accomplish?" If our objective is to build a family with close relationships with one another, then we should take the steps needed to build these relationships. If it is to have things, then we are free to invest an exorbitant amount of time away from our family, at work, building our salary, career or business. Each person must decide in his own heart the amount of time and effort that should be spent on acquiring the resources needed for the lifestyle that is right for them.

While giving financial seminars in economically depressed communities, I have learned that many people consider themselves victims. They believe they have no control over their income. Basic questions during our time together generally reveal that people who feel victimized should actively look for employment, show up for work on time, be productive at the work place and stop blaming others for their failure. Some find it is more profitable to take a government check than to work. Others look at their mental, physical abilities and social skills and determine that they do not have the capacity to care for themselves. But the Scriptures are clear in condemning individuals who are lazy and choose not to provide for themselves financially. Proverbs 10:26 states, *"Like vinegar to the teeth and smoke to the eyes, so is he sluggard to those who send him."* (ESV). The responsibility for our financial health rests on each of us. As individuals, we need to take stock of what we can do today in order to secure the income and lifestyle that brings the kind of balance we believe God intends for us.

Western culture currently provides the opportunity to decide to a large extent what we want our income to be. Influence over our income is based on what we choose to do for a living, how we spend our money, how we save, and how much time we spend working. It is true that some people are not receiving the income they believe they should have. Such people need to retool their skills so they have proficiency in areas that are attractive to potential employers. Others need to fashion a business plan to start a business or to move to a part of the country that is fertile with opportunities that fit them. Regardless, people have a great deal of control over their income. Sometimes the job that is available to them may not be something they enjoy or that brings the amount of money they desire, but, even in difficult economic times, opportunities abound. As my friends Buffy Bowman observed, "10% unemployment means that 90% of the people who want a job are able to find work."

An important question for each family to address is, *"What are we trying to accomplish with our income and employment?"* Are we working to secure money in order to develop a certain lifestyle, to build deep family relationships, give to charity, pay off bills, invest for the future, build a business, raise Godly children, have the nicest home possible, build a career, or gain money for the sake of having as much as possible? These questions deserve serious thought and conversation. Our conclusion influences the way we use our time and the resources available for the various categories in the budget. Priorities will be different for each person and family. The goal for each one should be to live the lifestyle they believe God has in mind for them or be changed to meet family preferences.

Housing (35 – 38%)

Financial experts recommend that housing costs including utilities should run between 35-38% of income (*"Affordable Housing" in Home and Community, a publication of the U.S. Department of Housing and Urban Development, December 15, 2010*) or 40% if you don't own a car. Homeowners will find it is generally recommended that a minimum of 10% of the mortgage cost should be designated to upkeep. If, for example, the monthly mortgage payment is $1,000 per month, $100 per month will be needed for home maintenance. Since a bag of lawn fertilizer costs $35 and a spreader to disperse the fertilizer costs another $50, lawnmowers cost between $100 and $2,800; $100 can disappear quickly. Even in a new house, things tend to need fixing.

Part of the reason our economy went into an economic slide in the latter part of the first decade of this century was because people were persuaded to buy houses they could not afford. Often, people were not required to put a down payment on their purchase and some optimistically purchased more home than they could afford or would have qualified for just a few years earlier. Realtors and loan salespeople who earned commissions based upon the value of the house or mortgage encouraged families to stretch themselves to secure the most expensive homes they could qualify to purchase. When these people extended themselves financially and purchased the more expensive homes, the realtor and loan officer received larger commissions. When the repercussions of the economic downturn began to be felt, companies began to down size, laying off people or cutting back employee hours. As a result, many families were unable to make their house payments. The hundreds of thousands of foreclosures caused economic chaos for the country, many failed businesses, and most importantly, extreme hardship and stress for the families who were displaced.

A lesson learned from this calamity is, when purchasing a house or renting an apartment, it is wise to be very conservative. Secure something you know you can afford, even if you encounter economically difficult times. Look at the amount you will pay each month and think about how it will impact your lifestyle. Don't allow the realtor, mortgage company, or your family to talk you into the unwise decision of stretching yourself financially and buying more home than you can afford. After all, *you* are the person who may have to live in a house without furniture or find yourself unable to purchase nice clothes or to go on vacation. You will be the one who stays awake at night worrying about your finances because you have overextended yourself. It is no fun to be "house poor" and unable to enjoy a balanced life. The rule to keep your house payment and utilities within the parameters listed here may result in a more humble home than you desire, but a balanced, stress-free lifestyle will be proof of the value of the decision. As equity builds in your current home and cash flow increases from employment, you may eventually be able to afford a nicer place and ultimately the dream house you desire.

I am often asked if a family should rent or buy. Many families see a home purchase as a way of building financial equity, but buying a house is more than just a financial investment; it also has a huge impact on time. The young couple going to school part-time and working full-time will find home ownership a significant challenge. When counseling young married couples, I encourage them to work on their relationship first. Spending time together building memories and developing their relationship is their most important priority. Of course, some find that working on their house and making plans for how they would like it to look, brings them closer together. Before you decide to buy, think through the effects homeownership may have on your relationships and your lifestyle.

Renting, of course, also costs money, but it usually has fewer expenses and requires less time on maintenance. This frees time and money so they can be used in other areas. My friend, Lionel Edwards, used to own a seventeen-room historic house built in 1817. He loved the house and found it served him and his wife well as they raised their family, but it took a great deal of time and expense to maintain. Lionel is a physician who serves as a consultant for pharmaceutical companies and also enjoys teaching at the graduate level. These professional activities require long, yet enjoyable hours. When his youngest child left, he and his wife sold their beautiful historic home and bought a two-bedroom condo with two offices. Maintenance of the yard and home are now taken care of by a professional staff. He has found that owning his condo is like renting, in that maintenance is no longer required of him. With the pressure of maintaining his historic house gone, he now has freedom to focus on his teaching and consulting. As Lionel puts it, "These are productive times for the Edwards family."

When making the decision to buy or rent, a family should consider first the impact the decision will have on the time left for family interaction and then choose the best balance of time and expenditures for this time in life. For some, buying a home is the wisest thing to do; for others, renting will work best, and still others may find that downsizing is the most logical approach. Remember, even if you have a fixed-payment mortgage, your taxes and insurance will go up over time.

Renting is a way of life for a large portion of the American population. For some, the time may come when they decide to buy a house. Traditionally, homebuyers have been told they needed to put 20% down at the time of purchase. The primary reasons for the down payment are twofold. First, it insures the purchaser has a significant commitment to pay off the mortgage. Homeowners show a greater commitment to pay their loan when they have placed tens of thousands of hard earned dollars into the house, and they know they will lose this money if there is a foreclosure. Second, a 20% down payment demonstrates the buyers have the discipline needed to save money and be financially responsible. Finding ways to avoid paying that 20% up front may seem beneficial to the person eager to buy a house. It is not unusual for someone to turn to family members to help with the down payment by loaning the money to them, but this circumvents the reason the 20% is required, and borrowing from family has the potential for straining otherwise wonderful family relationships.

Part of the traditional American Dream is to purchase a small house that fits well within the budget guidelines. As equity builds in the home and the family achieves greater income, they are able to place a healthy down payment on a nicer home. This process can repeat itself until, over time, the family reaches a level in which they are satisfied. The rule to remember is that it is important to determine your goals. Ask yourself what it is you are trying to accomplish and what kind of home you need to achieve your objectives. Is your intent to achieve a certain lifestyle and to build healthy relationships, or is it to reach some other goal? Determine first what you wish to accomplish and then purchase a home that will help you reach that goal.

Food: Tips for Saving Money on Groceries (15%)

Linda Brennan is a dear friend known for being a very smart shopper. Having raised two boys and as the wife of an InFaith missionary, she has gained insights on how the average family can make the most of their family dollars. She has some great tips for saving money on groceries. She provided the following insights:

> 1. It is important to have a general idea on how to feed your family well, even on a frugal budget. One of the easiest ways to save is to use the recourses already made available to you, such as coupons and store specials. Being intentional in taking advantage of coupons that come in the mail weekly or that you find online, and watching for specials, can save you money. When using coupons, be sure to compare prices. Sometimes you will pay less on a comparable brand than you would pay for a brand on sale, even when using a coupon.

> 2. Some suggest avoiding high-end stores, but rather go to a store that sells in bulk or is known for lesser prices. However, high-end stores sometimes have wonderful bargains, though you always need to *watch the prices* and compare. Grocery stores sometimes use good bargains (called "loss leaders") to get you into the store.

> 3. Unit pricing is very important. Check the tag on the shelf to learn the price per pound or price per unit. Sometimes it appears that buying a bigger package will be a better deal than buying a smaller package, but by checking the price per unit a lower price may be identified by buying the smaller package.

> 4. Warehouse clubs typically require shoppers to purchase large quantities. This can be an issue if the bulk purchase is not

used before the expiration date. If the product must be thrown out you will lose money even if you get a lower per-unit price. Some families get together with a group of other families or friends to shop at these stores. They split the costs, and divide the food so they can take advantage of the savings and use all of the product before the expiration date.

5. It is helpful to consider store brands. Sometimes they are actually the better product. They are often excellent in quality and have a lower price. I buy Store Brand detergent for $2.50. The same amount of Name Brand costs $14.00, and my clothes look as good as they would if I had purchased the Name Brand. I used to be a little stuck up about buying store brands. I would only buy Name Brand mayonnaise because I grew up believing it was the best, but I tried Store Brand mayonnaise, and it's pretty close. Try a store brand for each product, and if you don't like it, don't buy it again. You're wasting money if your family won't eat it.

6. I rarely buy anything at a grocery store that isn't food. The reason is price. The next time you walk through your local grocery store, take notice that less than half of the store has food items. The non-grocery items that take up more than half the store are there for your convenience and are priced slightly higher then elsewhere.. For example, motor oil costs twice as much; power cords, light bulbs, and cleaning products are not at optimal prices. The rule of thumb is to purchase hardware items at the hardware store and groceries at the grocery store if you want the best prices.

7. Some people find it helpful to carry a notebook in which to record prices as they visit various stores or check prices online. They can then compare prices and know with confidence they are getting the best deal.

8. Some people ask if prescriptions and over-the-counter drugs are less at the grocery store. I suggest checking the price lists that many stores publish. You can sometimes get these lists online. Some medications at discount stores are even less than if you use your insurance co-pay at a pharmacy.

9. Some items are not a wise purchase regardless of where you shop. Bottled water is a great example. While convenient, bottled water is typically the same stuff you get out of your tap at home. If you are concerned about the quality of the water your family drinks, purchase a water filter and place it on your kitchen faucet. The amount of money filtered water costs per unit is significantly lower than the price paid for bottled water.

10. Foundational for saving money at the store is drafting a menu. Purchases can then be made based on a shopping list based on your menu. Some people work out their menu ten days ahead, or even a month. As a result they don't have to shop as frequently. The less time spent in the store, the less the opportunity to spend money. We tend to plan our menu about six or seven days in advance. I look at grocery store fliers to see what is on special and work those bargains into the plan. We have a lot of pasta dishes and meatless casseroles on our menu and eat very little beef. It is also, important to know what you already have in your pantry. When you make your shopping list, try to stick to it. I say, "try to" stick to it because, sometimes, if you splurge on an item or two that you find on sale, it is a way to reward yourself, though regularly making impulsive buys can be a budget buster.

11. Don't go grocery shopping when you are hungry. Low blood sugar in your body will influence your purchases – when you are hungry, everything looks tasty, and you are more likely to make more impulsive buys. Hunger is not your friend and can influence your shopping decisions, and you will end up purchasing more than you intended.

12. Fast food has become a staple in our culture. Fast food meals are convenient and save a lot of time, especially for families who are busy running their kids from one activity to another, but for a family of five, one fast-food meal can easily add up to $20 or $30. We sometimes use coupons for fast-food, but I recommend avoiding fast-food as much as possible. Some good alternatives are to prepare meals ahead of time and place them in the freezer. You can take them out to defrost early in the day and then pop them in the oven to heat up quickly when ready. Also, store purchased prepared foods, like fast-food, will tend to be more expensive. It may seem more like a home cooked meal, and all you have to do is pop it in the oven like a meal you prepared ahead of time yourself, but it is typically much more expensive than the individual ingredients you need to make the dish yourself. Also, eat leftovers. My husband Loren takes the leftovers from dinner to work for lunch the next day. He saves us the cost of an additional meal by eating the leftovers.

Incorporating these money saving strategies and alternatives into your daily or weekly routine will pay off. Changes in spending habits, especially when it comes to feeding your family, may be hard to make but, when accomplished, you will see positive results on your budget and even in your family's wellbeing.

Summary: Tips for Saving Money on Groceries

* Stick with a shopping list.
* Don't buy anything on impulse.
* Avoid buying when you are hungry.
* Evaluate where to buy non-food items.
* Shop advertised specials.
* Use coupons to your advantage.

Clothing (5%)

Years ago, I read the book <u>Dress for Success</u>, in which the author, John T. Molloy, discussed a series of steps designed to help readers make wise decisions when shopping for clothes. The primary premise for the book was to provide insight into the processes for selecting and purchasing the appropriate clothes for various occasions. He emphasized that people should understand what clothing means to them and how the style they choose influences the thoughts and actions of others toward them. He taught that social status and general occupation is identified in part by the clothes worn. Children wear a different style than teenagers who wear different styles than middle aged people. Blue collar workers typically wear different styles than white collar employees. Red necks dress differently than blue bloods. While our approach to clothing in this chapter does not focus on the socioeconomic dimension of attire, an understanding of the impact of clothes socially should be addressed. After all, before any clothing purchase is made, the consumer should ask, "Do I really *need* it (for work, school or play), is it something I don't need but *want* or am I purchasing this because I *desire* it or just enjoy the shopping experience?"

The purchase of shoes provides a fitting example of these three questions. Some people see shoes as utilitarian and buy only what is practical, well made and comfortable. They contemplate what they need for work, home and play. How their shoes look is of little consequence. They *need* something functional and that is what they purchase. Others see shoes as a statement of fashion that reflects on them personally. They spend a great deal of time selecting the right shoe to fit various occasions. They may have many pair of dress as well as casual shoes from which to choose. They do not need this many shoes but *want* them because of the intrinsic value they bring. Others love shopping and find the selection of the right shoe at the right price in the right store to be a challenge they enjoy. During a recent counseling session, my client was distraught over her financial situation. Fearful that she was soon to be evicted from her home, we began to crunch the numbers in her budget. A line item that stood out was money for shoes. She loved shoes, had dozens of pairs and made it a point to buy several each month. She *desired* shoes, and her obsession played deeply into her financial dilemma. It was after thoughtful counsel and discussion about the importance of an accountability partner, who would keep a watchful eye over her future purchases, that we were able to design a reasonable Financial Plan.

This difference between needs, wants and desires should play into buying decisions. It is okay to want or desire clothes as long as the impact on the financial plan can be justified. Each purchase should be carefully scrutinized. Something that works well in making smart budgetary decisions is to: 1) write down a list of clothing items that need to be purchased, 2) indicate on the list the approximate amount to be designated to the purchase of the item and, 3) carry the list with you. If you see something on sale, you can see if it matches the items you have indicated you need. If the sale item is not on your list then it is not needed and therefore should not be purchased.

This list should reflect the resources you have designated in your annual and monthly budget for this expense. If you put your monthly allotment of money in an envelope, you can visually see what you can spend. When you find an item on your list, you can reach into the envelope and retrieve the cash set aside for the purchase.

Be aware of the best times to buy. Seasonal sales can work in your favor. The best time to buy a wool coat is in the middle or end of winter after everyone else has purchased their coats for the year and the store desires to reduce their stock and begin displaying clothes for the spring. A great time to purchase a bathing suit is mid-way through the summer or in August when everyone else has made their purchases and prices are now at their lowest. Purchasing at the middle or end of the season puts you ahead of everyone else. You have made purchases for the upcoming year as much as ten months ahead of everyone else.

It is, of course, important to be alert for *true* sales. Just because an item is marked down does not make it a sale for you. Know what it costs at other stores. If the sale price is still more than what you would pay somewhere else, it may be a sale for that store but not for you. My friend Andy invited me to a sale at the designer store where he works. Prices, he said, were as much as 50% off and right he was. A cotton shirt that regularly sold for $550.00 was marked down to $225.00. A beautiful sports jacket that generally sold for $1,300.00 was just $800.00 and a suit that was originally priced at $8,400.00 was just $4,000.00. Ties were as low as $125.00 and slacks just $185.00. These were truly sales for that store. Unfortunately, the prices still exceeded my budget, and I had to inform Andy that $25.00 for a pair of socks was more than I felt comfortable spending.

Taking care to watch prices at department stores or retailers that specialize in designer brands at lower prices, often due to manufacturers' overstocks or cleared-out seasonal inventory, can provide great savings. Know your prices and keep your list of needed clothes handy. Use this list as your buying guide when you encounter a sale.

Some families find an informal clothes exchange valuable. They join with other families with children and hand-down clothing to one another. When a child outgrows clothes that are still in pristine condition, they pass the item on to other families who can use them. It is a great way to save money and build friendships. Let others with children know that you are interested in receiving and passing along clothing.

Thrift shops are also a source of clothing for some. Clothing that has rarely been worn and sometimes clothes with the original price tag still attached can be found. While conducting a seminar at my home church, a woman with five children approached me with a confession. She politely conveyed that on Thursday evenings she and her family embark on an outing to the Salvation Army store. "Sometimes," she apologetically confessed, "the prices are so good, I allow my children to exceed their individual budgets." Her children were well dressed in their thrift shop clothes. To overcome the temptation to spend more than her budget allowed in the future, we developed a plan in which she gave each child an envelope with cash. They were allowed to spend the money allotted to them, but no more. As a result, they learned financial responsibility and how to make good purchasing decisions.

Transportation (10%)

When we think of transportation, most people think of automobiles. However, this section is identified as transportation, not automobiles in order to help us focus on what it is we are trying to accomplish. After all, our decisions as to how we travel have deep ramifications into many aspects of our lives. The level of accessibility, flexibility, style, mode and cost, each impact our lives. Many people live in large cities where cars are more trouble than of value. People take the bus, taxi, town car or subway quickly and efficiently. If they need to go out of town they simply rent a car for the day. Suburbanites and people who live in rural areas, on the other hand, have lifestyles that require the independent transport that a car allows. My argument is that we need to take an objective look at what it is we desire to accomplish before settling on a mode of transportation. Is a bus optimal or would a bicycle serve the purpose better? Do we need a motorcycle or will a van or SUV fit our family best? Is our purpose to safely get from Point A to Point B or are we buying a status symbol or making a lifestyle statement by the mode of transportation we choose? Are we at a point where we can buy a car that is fun to drive, or must our decision be all about how well the machine functions? The choices we make in transportation will impact our budget and our lifestyle. Most people find the convenience of an automobile fits their lifestyle well. The freedom to commute when and where they desire is attractive to them.

The recommended amount to designate toward transportation on the budget percentage sheet is 11-15%. This percentage includes the monthly car payment, insurance, repairs and maintenance, gas, tolls, registrations and licenses. As a general guideline, when purchasing a car, pay cash. If you do need to take out a loan, pay if off as quickly as possible and have a celebration when the last payment is made. After your celebration, begin saving for your next car by putting into savings the amount of your current monthly payment. You will still be making a car payment, but you are now paying yourself and keeping the interest instead of giving it to someone else.

When the time comes to make this purchase, there are ten guidelines that will help make a wise choice.

Basic Steps for Purchasing an Automobile

1. Slow down and take your time.
2. Know what you need or want.
3. Consider a pre-owned car.
4. Budget before you shop.
5. Pay cash if you can.
6. Arrange financing first.
7. Do your homework.
8. Don't buy on your first visit.
9. Never leave a deposit until the seller has agreed to your price.
10. Don't trade in your old car.

---

1. Slow down and take your time. If you feel anxious about your decision and pressured to buy a particular car, stop the process immediately and walk away. Chances are you are not making a wise decision. When you rush to buy, the salesperson and your heart will influence you. Buy with your head. Salesmen attend formal training sessions designed to teach them how to make you feel you must buy today or "you will miss the deal." This is an artificial environment contrived to sway your emotions. When you feel this way, remember you are in charge of your life. The truth is you don't need this deal. There are many other great cars and great deals out there that are just as good as this one. Time is on your side and buying a car is a major decision. Be patient, shop around, gather information, do your research and then make an informed, rational decision.

2. *Know what you need or want.* Ask yourself, "Am I looking for transportation, convenience, utility, fun, status or a combination of all of the above?" Be honest about your intent and then endeavor to make a logical decision. Prioritize the qualities and features that are important to you. Write down what you: 1) must have and cannot live without, 2) would like to have, and 3) think would be nice but are not important. Include brand, price, warranty, size, color, options, etc. For some, features such as air conditioning, a radio, bucket seats, four-wheel drive, seating for eight, large cargo capacity, style and quality matter. Other people find these options of little interest.

3. *Consider a pre-owned car.* Also to be considered is whether a new car or a pre-owned car is less expensive and more practical in the long run. The answer, of course, depends on many factors. Most notably, it depends on the quality of the car, but you can often buy a well-built used car with low mileage for much less than a comparable new model. Typical repair costs of the model you are considering are readily available "on line" as are major areas of concern. Services are also available that will show the individual repair history on most cars. It is not uncommon for a person to lease a car for three years only to turn it into the dealer with extremely low miles and in pristine condition. Many of these cars are certified by the dealer and guaranteed for as many as 100,000 miles. Individuals on a tight budget might consider purchasing their car from a private party. When doing such, learn all you can about the brand and model by searching the web. I highly recommend taking the car to a mechanic you feel you can trust so they can point out areas of concern. Knowing the condition of a car before making the purchase allows you to offer a fair price and to walk away aware of the liabilities associated with your purchase. The more the miles, the greater the chance you will have repairs. Most cars will run between 150,000 and 200,000 miles before they need a major repair. My approach has been to keep my cars until they become unsafe, or the repair bills exceed what the monthly payments would be. Of course, my wife's car has over 230,000 at this point. We recognize there are many small issues and are waiting patiently for a large expensive repair that will demand we

dip into our savings to pay either for the large repair or to purchase a replacement car. All cars eventually wear out and must be replaced.

4. *Budget before you shop.* Know what you can afford and how much you are willing to pay. Once that decision is made, stick to your decision. If the seller asks you what you are looking to spend, do not answer the question. Talk instead about the quality, miles and features you expect. You will show you have done your homework and have established your level of expectation. Some dealers train their sales staff to ask customers how much they can afford to pay each month. This allows them to push for extending payments for long periods of time enticing you to spend more than you intended and for a much greater period of time. The longer the payment period, the more the buyer will spend on interest. Price is something that is generally posted and you can step away from those cars that are outside your price range.

5. *Pay cash if you can.* You have learned to budget and in doing such, you have paid off your current car. Once the car is paid for, continue making payments to yourself. After several years of making car payments into your own savings account, you will have saved enough money to purchase a good used car for cash. When you pay cash you only make one payment for the car. As stated above, begin immediately the process of making payments to yourself for your next car. Saving up ahead of time removes the pressure and fear of missing a payment and creates an additional source of funds when emergencies arise.

6. *Arrange financing first.* Sometimes the money you have set aside for a car is not sufficient for the one you desire. Before physically looking at cars, go to your bank or credit union and discuss what kind of deal they can offer you. Once you know the interest rate, the approximate amount of money you can delegate toward payments in your budget and the number of months you desire to pay, then look at specific cars. With this knowledge in hand, you will know specifically what you can afford to spend and will be better able to negotiate a

price that fits your budget. If you are at a dealer and he offers you a better interest rate, you can take the deal. On the other hand, if his financing is higher than your bank or credit union you will be able to write him a check for the full amount of the car. If you buy through a private party, you will have the money on reserve and be able to write a check at will. The focus of your attention will be on the car, not on financing.

7. *Do your homework.* Use the web, books, and magazines to learn all about the kinds of cars that fit your needs before you look at specific models. Research the positives and negatives. What does it cost to run per year? What is its repair history? Identify their features, the maintenance schedule and location of dealers or repair shops near you.

8. *Don't buy on your first visit.* You need time to think and so does the dealer. If there is not a repair history printout for a used vehicle, get one during this time. A car purchase is a big decision that you need to consider and discuss. Take the time to do that.

9. *Never leave a deposit until the seller has agreed to your price.* A deposit is the hook that commits you to the deal. The seller has you psychologically. If you decide against the car after you leave, you will need to go back to the salesman and ask for your check. He will then have the opportunity to lure you into another "once in a lifetime" deal. Establish the attitude that, "If someone else purchases the car when you are at home contemplating the purchase, good for them. Apparently this was the car meant for them, not for you." You now have the opportunity to look for a different car that will possibly better meet your needs. There is no perfect car for you and your family. There are, however, many cars that will adequately meet your transportation needs.

10. *Don't trade in your old car.* You will not get the best price if you trade your car into the dealer. Of course, you may be willing to get less for the trade-in due to the hassle involved with selling it yourself. After all, selling a well-used car requires time, expense, and

inconvenience. You must be willing to speak with people, display ads, spread the news by bothering your friends and you must be patient. However, if you are willing to sell the car yourself you have the opportunity to make the best profit.

Life Insurance (5%)

> If anyone does not provide for his relatives, and
> especially for his immediate family, he has denied the faith
> and is worse than an unbeliever.
> - 1 Timothy 5:8 (NIV)

What will happen to your family when you die? How will they survive financially? Will they have the resources they need to live comfortably when you are no longer able to contribute as you do today? These are very real questions that each person needs to address. According to 1 Timothy 5:8, we are each responsible to provide for our immediate family. This responsibility extends beyond our lifetime as they will be counting on us even when we are gone.

How this plays out is of course different for everyone. If you are single or half of an older retired couple with a substantial nest egg, you may not need life insurance. After all, no one is relying on you for income. The only money you will need after you die is what is required for your burial. But if your family is counting on you for provisions, you may need insurance to help carry them through a period of time without the income you provide. When purchasing life insurance, it is important to determine what it is you are trying to accomplish and secure a policy that allows you to meet that need.

The question is often asked, "Is whole-life insurance best or should I buy term insurance?" There are of course advantages to both. Simply stated, term insurance is less expensive but, once premiums stop, so does the coverage. With whole life, a person gains value in the policy and if at some point the policyholder stops making premium payments, the payout benefit will continue based on a preset formula determined by the amount previously paid into the policy. It is important to know that life insurance should be purchased as a means by which to help others in the event of the policyholder's death. It is not in itself a good investment. Some sales people will promote their product as a good investment but please note: "Only an insurance salesperson will tell you that life insurance is a good investment instrument." This is because they make money on each sale. Purchase life insurance to provide for your family if you die. Invest your money for the future through other traditional investment instruments.

How much insurance do you need? A good rule of thumb for a married person with a family is to be insured for ten times your annual income plus enough to pay off debts, including your house. This amount will remove house payments from your family, take care of funeral expenses and pay for some services you might have provided yourself such as home maintenance, auto repair, tax preparation, tune-ups, cooking, and child care. Some people will find this amount a bit aggressive and costly. Take time and consider carefully the condition your family will be in if you die, and purchase the amount needed to secure for them what they need as they continue through life without you. The decision should be made logically without emotion as it is a long-term commitment and has implications on your monthly budget.

Entertainment / Vacations (5%)
Years ago, when working as a Registered Nurse, I had a patient, Mrs. Toliver, who had been married for fifty-three years. According to Mrs. Toliver, she had a wonderful marriage and was saddened by the death of her husband. One day I asked, "Mrs. Toliver, what was the key to your very happy marriage?"

She looked at me and without hesitation shared her secret. She said, "Honey, never go to bed mad. Say you love your spouse every day, buy your wife flowers once a week, and have a date once a month." These were the things that she found of meaning as she looked back over her time with her husband. Flowers and a date cost money and she and her husband were poor, but in their relationship, they felt the expense was well worth the investment. These things represented the love she and her husband had together and created fond memories. Now, I am not a big advocate for eating out often, because it is an expense that creates financial havoc for many couples, and flowers can be expensive. However, a date once a month is something to look forward to and does not need to involve spending lots of cash. Recreation is an activity meant to re-create or renew. Activities that can do this need to be given priority and therefore listed as a budget item.

Ideas couples have shared with me for spending time together have included joining a church volleyball league, taking walks by the river, attending neighborhood sporting events, going to the community theater, or visiting with friends and neighbors. The intent is to create memories that are cherished and which refresh and revitalize. The amount that can be budgeted for recreation and vacations may be austere for some initially, only to take on a new significance later. Vacations for some families with whom I have worked have ranged from a day at the beach to two weeks in London and a month in Hawaii. The point is to designate some money each month for recreation and vacations and to use this money to reach your desired intent.

The question to ask is this, "When you are lying in bed at the end of your life, what will you remember? Family vacations? Fun things you did with your spouse? What memories will you want to have made?" Now, go make those memories.

Discussion Questions and Assignments:

1. Consider carefully the lifestyle you believe God has in mind for you now. Write down the number of work hours, income level, training and effort that is required for you to accomplish this. Does this reflect a healthy balance? How might the time and effort required for you to achieve this standard of living be different now than four years in the future? What struggles does this present?

2. What are you trying to accomplish with your desired income and lifestyle? What is your goal?

3. It is recommended that a house be purchased only when a minimum of 20% of the price be made as the down payment and the mortgage and utilities do not exceed 35% of the monthly budget. Explain the rationale for these recommendations.

4. Under what conditions is it better to rent than to purchase a home?

5. Describe four of the best steps you can take to save money on food purchases. Include the use of a menu as one of your choices.

6. The difference between needs, wants and desires are described in this chapter. Give examples of several purchases that might be different if these three distinctions were considered before making a purchase.

7. Review the insights presented on the purchase of clothing. Which do you find most helpful? What other suggestions do you have for making wise decisions when buying clothes?

8. Review the ten guidelines for purchasing an automobile. Which of the ten stand out to you as the most significant? Explain.

9. What is the biblical justification for life insurance? How much life insurance should you have? Explain your reasoning.

10. Provide a list of benefits associated with budgeting time and money for recreation and hobbies.

Chapter 6: Finding Money You never Knew You Had

A friend of mine, Ron Emburg, was a missionary with the mission organization now known as InFaith. Before becoming a missionary he owned several very successful businesses. By nature, Ron seemed to have an uncanny insight into making and saving money. Learning to live on a missionary's income, he developed further the art of frugality. His friends looked to him as a person able to stretch a dollar further than anyone else.

One day, Ron said to me, "Bryce, I've discovered something wonderful – I have learned exactly how much toothpaste to put on a toothbrush!" Taken aback by this odd discovery, I was interested in his insight. He went on to explain that on television ads, they spread a large amount of toothpaste across the entire top of the toothbrush. His experience was that if he used that much toothpaste, most of it fell into the sink as he turned his toothbrush to put it to his lips. So his question was, "How much toothpaste do you really need?" Ron experimented by covering just half of his toothbrush. He then tried a quarter, and then an eighth. He concluded that a person needs only to cover about a quarter of the toothbrush to obtain the suds needed for shiny, clean teeth. He surmised that if a family is paying $3 each month for toothpaste and they are able to cut the use down by 75%, they would only be paying 75 cents, saving $2.25 each month. $2.25 times 12 months is $27 per year. Now, $2.25 a month or $27 a year might not sound like much to some people, but if I were to hand you $27, chances are you would accept it gladly. The principle is that saving a little each month can add up to a lot over the year. When applied to a number of other areas of daily spending, these small savings can add up to a tremendous amount.

One popular example of how we often spend money without realizing its impact on our lives is through the purchase of coffee. If a person pays $5.00 for a latte at their favorite coffee shop before work each weekday, another while hanging out with friends on Saturday, and still Another after church on Sunday, they will spend $35 each week or $1,825 on coffee over the course of a year ($5.00 X 365 days = $1,825). If asked whether they would like to have an extra $1,825, most people would say, "Absolutely! How can I do that?" The answer for many is simple: make your own coffee at home for a fraction of what you are paying at the coffee shop. The 50 cents it costs to make a latte at home ($.50 x 365 = $182.50) is a savings of $4.50 per day, or a savings of $1,642.50 per year.

At one time I worked at a local hospital and would often eat lunch in the nurses' lounge with a group of my friends. Most of them would order out for a minimum of $7.50 each. I would pack a sandwich that cost me about 50 cents. I might be cheap, but $7.50 x 5 days x 50 weeks (excluding two weeks for vacation) = $1,875 a year. I was spending $0.50 x 5 x 50 weeks or $125 per year for lunch. To me, $1,875 was a lot of money, and I was interested in spending my money on my family. The savings of $1,750 per year ($1,875 - $125) was significant to me. Individuals who spend $7.50 on lunch each day ($1,875 per year) and $5 for coffee each day ($1,825 per year) may be saying, "I don't know where all my money is going. It seems like I don't have enough money to pay my basic bills." Had they made the two simple adjustments of making their own coffee and lunch they could have a total of $3,363.50 in savings ($1,750.00 lunch and $1,642.50 coffee).

Most people will find these expenses to be just the beginning. Add money spent on toothpaste, unnecessary use of electricity and other utilities, convenience foods, dining out, cable, and cell phone service and soon the compounding costs of these little things take on tremendous value.

Spending Snowflakes
During the winter season, when anticipating a snowstorm, the landscape displays a variety of colors. One by one snowflakes drift to the ground, and over a period of time the landscape turns completely white with a heavy blanket of snow. Small, individual daily purchases are like these "snowflakes." They drift in one by one, each one seemingly innocent on its own, but soon our financial landscape is covered. Each *spending snowflake* represents a single financial decision that, joining with many other small decisions made over time, results in a changed financial landscape. Imagine putting on a pair of "snowflake glasses" that would allow you to spot and redirect those *spending snowflakes* before they land. What bills could you pay or debts could you remove with the money you would find? $3,363.50 a year can go a long way to pay for a vacation, remove a debt, increase savings for a down payment on a house, or stash money away for retirement or emergencies. Added with savings from other changes in spending, this money can provide additional resources so you can focus on what is truly important to you. Yes, looking at the world from the perspective of "How can I save money?" instead of "How can I spend money for self gratification?" can make a big difference.

In his book, The Millionaire Next Door, author Thomas J. Stanley reveals that most people who have millionaire status are not the people we typically stereotype as having money. The average millionaire – that is, someone who has more than a million dollars in investments beyond the value of his or her home – is typically a hard-working person who has lived a relatively frugal life, saving money consistently over time. Millionaires usually are not the people who dine out excessively at high-end restaurants, buy new luxury cars, and wear the latest fashion from expensive stores, or who purchase items daily for immediate self-gratification. Rather, they are individuals who wear "snowflake glasses" that allow them to the see the big picture and make purchases based on a balanced view of both immediate and long-term financial and lifestyle objectives. The key here is the word "balanced." Completely denying all extravagance is not compelling for most people, but the family who identifies areas where they can find money to use for what is truly important to them is able to make informed decisions that meet their long-range goals. The answer is to carefully determine family priorities and to spend money in those areas that support these priorities.

The way we spend money today influences how much we have left to spend tomorrow. Viewing finances from the vantage of snowflake glasses is a great asset in improving your financial condition. Once you start looking for *spending snowflakes* around you, you will be able to find many new ways to save. The list of money saving tips below will help you get started in finding money you never knew you had available to you.

Many families have found that a family meeting designed to explore ideas for saving money, or a family contest in which family members brainstorm ideas for saving money, and giving a prize to the person or team who comes up with the most ideas, can be a bonding exercise. Suggestions may include not using so much toilet paper, drinking tap water instead of soda, turning out lights when leaving a room, lowering the temperature in the winter and raising the temperature in summer, or making birthday gifts for one another instead of purchasing them. Having family interaction, such as a contest or discussions, will bring suggestions that are tailored to fit the personality of your particular family. Some suggestions may have to be modified so they are practical and fit your family in a practical manner. The junior-high boy, for example, might suggest he save on hot water by only showering once a week, or to save on toothpaste, he may volunteer to stop brushing his teeth all together. "After all," he may argue, "I am just trying to comply with the family objective of 'finding money we never knew we had.'" Such suggestions will be curbed by a loving parent.

Whatever your family decides to do, the ideas below are designed to get you started in thinking about ways you can alter your actual spending habits to save more. Others exist on various websites and in other books on frugality and personal finance.

115 Ways to Save Money
Use it up; wear it out; make it do; or do without!

Cell Phones
1. Get a flat-rate plan.
2. If your contract has expired, call the cell phone company and ask for better rates.
3. Stuck in a bad contract? Call the company and renegotiate.
4. Compare pre-paid cell phone plans (and the small print) before you buy.
5. Downgrade your plan to fewer minutes if you are not using them all.
6. Eliminate your home landline.

Internet
1. Don't call 411 for directory assistance. Look up telephone numbers on free internet directories instead.
2. Search online for coupons and coupon codes.
3. Need car repairs? Check sites that offer fair prices for your area.
4. Inexpensively trade books, music CDs, and DVDs on internet sites
5. Check prices online before you buy.
6. Recycle all electronics for cash through online services.

Electric & Heat
1. Regularly clean or replace air conditioning and heating filters.
2. Compare electric providers and switch if it saves you dollars.
3. Find out if your electric company offers a plan that gives a lower rate for using electricity during off-peak hours. If so, run your dishwasher, washing machine, and dryer during those times.
4. Apply for federal (and state) weatherization programs.
5. Check your windows and doors for air leaks with a piece of burning incense.
6. Use motion sensors on light switches so they automatically go off when the room is empty.
7. Turn off fans (including ceiling fans) when you leave a room.

8. Install a timer on your electric hot water heater so it goes off during times in which you do not need hot water.
9. Use compact fluorescent, LCD, or other energy-saving light bulbs.
10. Take showers that last no longer than 5 minutes in length.
11. Ask your electric utility provider for a free energy audit.
12. Turn your thermostat down two degrees (maximum temperature of 68 degrees) in winter and up two degrees (minimum temperature of 72 degrees) in the summer.
13. Use a programmable thermostat so you are able to have better control of room temperature.
14. For extra heat, open the curtains on sunny days and keep them closed on overcast days; do the opposite to keep the house cool.
15. Do regular preventive maintenance on your appliances. Check filters, vents, and cooling coils on your air conditioner and refrigerator.

<u>Laundry</u>
1. Wash and rinse in cold or warm water—not hot.
2. Adjust your hot water to a maximum of 120 degrees.
3. Run your washer through an extra spin cycle at the end of a wash. See how much extra water is removed. This reduces the time needed to run the dryer.
4. Try using half the recommended amount of laundry detergent. Your clothes will typically be just as clean as using the recommended amount.
5. Remove clothes immediately when the dryer stops to reduce the need to iron. The iron uses a large amount of electricity.
6. Never run the washer with less than a full load of laundry.
7. Use a clothesline instead of an electric dryer.
8. Cut dryer sheets in half. A half sheet is just as effective as a full sheet.
9. Don't send anything to be dry-cleaned that can be washed at home.
10. Buy the detergent that is on sale, as there is little difference in efficiency.

Car

1. Drive 55 miles per hour or less. The faster you go, the more fuel you use.
2. Remove excess weight. Every 100 pounds of weight in the car reduces fuel efficiency by two additional miles per gallon.
3. Use cruise control to maintain an even speed, which in turn increases efficiency.
4. Turn off the car if you expect to idle for more than one minute.
5. Conduct auto maintenance according to manufacturers' guidelines.
6. Do your own maintenance and tune-ups, including replacing wiper blades, maintaining fluid levels, and changing the oil.
7. Check tire pressure regularly.
8. Combine auto and home insurance policies under the same company.
9. Identify all the insurance policy discounts that are available to you and raise the deductible.
10. Buy a late-model used car rather than a new one. A car typically loses 20-30% of its value as soon as it is driven off the lot.
11. If you are over 55, take the safe driver course and reduce your insurance premium.
12. Wash your car at home, not at the automatic carwash.
13. Remove roof and bike racks that are not being used. The difference in fuel efficiency can be as much as 6%.
14. Save gas by running several errands in one trip and planning your route so you don't have to backtrack.
15. Carpool when possible.

Clothes

1. Try store-brand disposable diapers instead of national brands.
2. Buy clothes at a thrift shop or yard sales. Many times they will still have the "new" tags on.
3. Repair damaged clothes instead of throwing them out.
4. Purchase clothes that mix and match well.
5. Purchase clothes at the end of the season, when clothes are on sale.
6. Make a list of what you need and keep the list with you so you can refer to it when you encounter a sale.

7. Buy school backpacks your kids can use for several years. (Be careful of age-related themes.)
8. Check for kids' clothes exchanges in your area or start one of your own with your friends.
9. Buy clothes that won't go out of style quickly.
10. Check online for sales and coupons from your favorite stores and brands.

Personal Care
1. Shop around for the best prices for your prescriptions and over-the-counter drugs.
2. Use generic drugs whenever possible.
3. Have a skilled friend or family cut your hair.
4. Use coupons and rebates on hygiene and personal care products.
5. Check out a book on home remedies from your library and learn how to save on hygiene products. For example, olive oil can soothe an achy ear, revive damaged hair, and smooth rough skin.
6. Make your own toothpaste out of baking soda and salt.
7. Purchase hygiene products at non-grocery stores. The price is typically lower.
8. Buy your eyeglasses and contacts online.
9. Don't pay to have your nails done.
10. Try less expensive store-brand products. They are often just as good as or better than name-brand products.

Cleaning Solutions and Stain Removers
1. All-purpose cleaner: ½ cup vinegar, ¼ cup baking soda, and ½ gallon water – use in a spray bottle.
2. Vinyl floor cleaner: 1 gallon warm water + 1 cup vinegar + a few drops of baby oil.
3. Use a small amount of paint thinner to remove oil stains on clothes.
4. Use a low-cost shampoo as a general cleaning solution.
5. Olive oil cleans stainless-steel surfaces.
6. Make your own laundry soap. Get the formula on the Internet.
7. Buy large bottles of bubble bath to use as hand soap.

Food

1. Make a shopping list based on your week's menu. Stick with your shopping list when in the store.
2. Plan your meals around what is on sale in your grocery store's flyer.
3. Use the unit pricing information located next to the price in your supermarket to determine the actual amount you are paying per piece or per ounce.
4. Beware of bulk items. Smaller packages may actually cost the same or less per ounce.
5. Compare items on sale with the price of similar items that are not on sale but are typically lower. Purchasing a less expensive substitute may be just as good and more frugal.
6. When contemplating the advantages of shopping at food warehouses enter the cost membership into your calculation.
7. Drink more tap water and less soda, expensive juices, bottled water, and milk.
8. Cut back on convenience foods, as they are costly. For example, precut salad is typically seven times more expensive than a head of iceberg lettuce.
9. Buy and use a crock-pot. They provide inexpensive, yet convenient, meals.
10. Pack your own lunch for work instead of purchasing lunch.
11. Pack food (snacks and meals) before leaving on a road trip.
12. Don't shop for food when you are hungry as hunger influences purchasing decisions.
13. Buy bottles of herbs and spices at an outlet or discount store.
14. Buy bags of frozen vegetables rather than boxes.
15. Make your own baby food.
16. Plant a garden.
17. If you are over 55 and eating at a fast-food restaurant, ask if they have a senior discount.
18. Eat out less frequently.
19. Shop late in the evening and ask the meat manager for discounted meats available at many grocery stores.

General Living

1. Never buy a lottery ticket. The lottery is called "the poor man's tax" because tickets are typically purchased by people who have little money to spend and who rarely win anything of significance. They are hoping for a better future, but they are essentially giving money away on false hope.
2. Give up smoking. It is expensive and provides few positive results.
3. Call service providers and other companies with whom you deal regularly to ask for suggestions on how you can save money. This tip is especially helpful for companies that provide cell phone subscriptions, newspaper delivery, Internet service, and cable TV.
4. If you need an expensive tool, try to borrow or rent one first. It can help you decide which features to look for if you then decide to buy.
5. Use your local library instead of buying books, CDs, DVDs, and videos.
6. Looking for a family outing? Read your community calendar to find free events, such as concerts and plays, or go on a picnic or visit a free museum for a family outing.
7. Clean out your closets. Have a yard sale and put the proceeds toward a family project.
8. Cancel unused club memberships.
9. Do your holiday shopping right after each holiday in preparation for the upcoming year.
10. Get rid of subscriptions to magazines that lie around unread.
11. Always ask for fees to be waived. You will be amazed at the savings.
12. Shop at the dollar store—but not for food or vitamins, as they may be near their expiration date.
13. Skip the service contract or extended warrantees on appliances. Typically, they are not cost efficient.
14. Challenge your property tax.
15. Contact manufacturers with complaints or compliments. Many send coupons or freebies to people who give them feedback.
16. Check for sports equipment exchanges in your area.
17. Travel in the off-season to get lower rates on lodging (and avoid crowds).

18. Avoid buying movies, music, books, and electronics when they are first released; wait for the prices to go down.

Remember – for more ideas, you can read personal finance blogs, or check out books at the library.

Out-of-Pocket Expenses

While saving money by wearing *snowflake glasses,* it is important to gain an understanding of the out-of-pocket expenses that generally fall into the Miscellaneous category of the budget. These expenses, if left unchecked, can be the demise of an otherwise healthy budget.

In a conversation with my friend, Chris, he expressed frustration over his use of cash. He said that on Monday morning he checked his wallet to make sure he had enough money to buy gas on the way to work and was surprised to find he only had $10. He asked his wife, Andrea, if she had borrowed anything from his wallet, and she said, "No, I never go into your wallet, and this weekend was no exception." The nearly "cash-free" wallet (that is, free from cash) seemed odd. Chris remembered going to the ATM after work on Friday and withdrawing $200, but he couldn't remember where it went. He felt cheated, almost as if someone had stolen money from him.

The crucial question was, "Where did he spend his money over the weekend?" After all, if he does not know where his money went, how can he manage it? After a short discussion with Andrea, Chris remembered that Friday evening he had treated the family to pizza. Saturday morning, he had gone to the men's breakfast at church, which had cost him $10, and had stopped at the grocery store on the way home to purchase milk, bread, and soda for Andrea. Later, he bought some gas for the lawnmower and purchased fertilizer for the yard. He had also bought a cup of coffee and a small book on hiking at the bookstore. The Monday morning cashless surprise is not uncommon, but it can be frustrating. How can the right amount of money be designated for various items in the budget if we are not sure of how much is being spent, where it is spent, and who is spending it?

Fortunately, there is a simple way to determine where our money goes. I have provided in this chapter a form designed to get a handle on discretionary or "out-of-pocket," expenses. On this form, the left-hand column is used to write the date a purchase is made, the middle column provides space to list the item purchased, and the right-hand column shows the amount spent. Portable notebooks with a variety of columns are available at most book stores for a nominal price. For technophiles, there are applications for your phone, as well as other electronic devices designed to meet this need.

In order to be effective, you must take the form or notebook wherever you go so you can record expenses immediately after paying. Experience dictates that many items will be forgotten if the form is left at home or in the car with the intent that it will be updated periodically. Living by the rule that you will not purchase any item unless you have this form (or an alternative) in hand will assure that all items are accounted for.

While I don't advocate using this form for the rest of your life, recording expenses for three months or more will provide a realistic understanding of where money is spent. Annually revisiting the form for a month or more will help refine an existing budget and provide an understanding of the spending process. When trying to make an accurate budget, each family member will know exactly where all of the out-of-pocket money went – how much was spent for groceries, gas, fast food, coffee, home repairs, etc.

A side benefit of using this form is that it typically helps people be more frugal. Writing down expenses provides the opportunity to think about what is being spent. In my experience, writing down each item at the time of purchase generally reduces the amount spent by 30% or more. This is especially true for the person who has a financial accountability partner. The financial accountability partner will review all budget expenses including out-of-pocket expenses and discuss whether each expense is rational and appropriate.

Out of Pocket Expenses

Date	Description of Expense	Amount

Practical Priorities

Many of the suggestions in the "115 Ways To Save Money" listed above sound like good ideas to the average reader. It may be that a long shower is worth the extra money, or that planting a garden does not fit a rushed urban lifestyle. For this reason, it is important to contemplate and discuss personal priorities with a financial accountability partner before completing a budget. It's not the big decisions, like how large the mortgage is going to be or the size of the car payment that couples tend to fight about, rather the little things, like turning off lights, taking long showers, and specific grocery purchases, which lead to verbal combat.

Imagine the husband who is in charge of paying the monthly electric bill coming home at the end of an extra long day to a house that appears to have all of its lights on. When he walks inside, he recognizes that his wife had been working in the master bedroom's closet and bathroom, had then walked down the hall into the den, continued downstairs to the kitchen to make a sandwich and finally, went to the family room to eat in front of the television. When she left each room, she had left the lights on and ultimately fell asleep in front of the television. The husband, having worked an extra long day to provide for his family, and having seen his wife fast asleep in a well-lit house, feels as if his extra effort is being squandered. It takes very little imagination to see a very intense discussion between these two regarding the expense of lighting rooms in which no one is present.

By the same token, the wife might prefer to save money on showers. She turns on the water, jumps in to get wet, turns off the water, suds up, turns the water back on, and rinses off. She uses about three minutes of water each day. But when her husband comes home, he looks forward to relaxing by taking a long, hot shower that steams up the bathroom and uses up all the water in the water tank. His long shower may be seen by her as an excessive use of hot water, and result in an intense family discussion about finances.

Arguments about these and other expenses can be avoided by deciding together what is right for your family. Resources are limited. Will money be spent on long, hot showers or saved by taking short showers and setting the water heater to a lower temperature? How warm should the house be in the winter and how cool in the summer months? Is it wise to plant a garden, should the family buy a membership to a food warehouse, and is it agreeable to purchase clothing at a thrift shop? Each family must decide what is right for them. The intent is to establish a lifestyle that the family can agree on so they can meet their life and financial objectives with the resources available.

Discussion Questions and Assignments:

1. What are snowflake glasses? How might this concept help a person find money they never knew they had?

2. Identify six items other than lunch, coffee and toothpaste that can provide you with increased income for use in areas that are important to you. Add up the money you can save by implementing these changes in spending.

3. It has been said that millionaires have different behaviors than people who have little in savings. What is the premise behind this statement?

4. 115 ways to save money are noted in this chapter. Identify an additional 12 ways to save money.

5. Describe the Out of Pocket Expenses Form as presented in this chapter. Put this form to work for at least one week. Identify what you learned as a result of your involvement with this tool.

6. It has been said that it is generally the small expenses most families fight about. Do you agree? Give a practical example to substantiate your answer.

7. Consider the challenges you have faced in implementing the Financial Plan introduced in Chapter 3. Identify what these are and what can be done to deal with them.

8. What are some of the insights you have learned about implementing your budget that you did not expect?

9. How has your conversations with your family or Accountability Partner about formulating and implementing your financial plan impacted you or your family?

10. The major complaint about formulating a budget is the lack of money to cover expenses. How have you dealt with this issue?

Chapter 7: Gaining Freedom from the Pressures of Debt

Frank and Barbara Bridge finally reached their financial and physical goals. Frank, at a stout 328 pounds desired to loose 100 pounds in 12 months. Barbara, in debt with her Credit Cards and frequent purchasing sprees ran up debt to over $16,750 with little to show for it. Together they made a covenant to curb their accesses. Frank, after a physical exam and consultation with his physician, began an arduous health program that included exercise and reduced calorie diet. Barbara, after taking inventory of outstanding obligations and establishing a lean budget for both personal and family expenses began the process of implementing her plan. Both Frank and Barbara faced similar challenges. Their plans required self-discipline, changes in daily habits, close attention to detail, consistency, and goal orientation. Neither the process of losing weight or becoming debt free is easy but the rewards of doing such can be life changing.

Imagine what it would feel like for you personally if you had no debts. Would you feel a sense of relief from many of the pressures that have taken hold of your life? Would life be less stressful? Would a feeling of relief fill your being? Would family discussions be less tense? Would the time you need to spend at work be lessened? Most people find a debt free life brings a fresh feeling of confidence and a sense of inner peace. Additionally, paying off debt can be a "fun process" if the entire family becomes involved. The system recommended in this chapter is simple, can be achieved by anyone, and provides multiple opportunities to "celebrate" with family and friends.

The first step is to complete the Debt Identification provided in the appendix of this chapter. This form provides a column on which to list debts. Next to that column, space is provided to identify the amount owed and the third column provides room to identify the amount paid monthly.

Once these are identified, the next step is to arrange them from the smallest amount owed to the largest. This list should include all debts including money borrowed for furniture, automobiles, credit cards, medical expenses, college loans, and mortgage as well as personal debts to friends and family. For this exercise, a debt is any loan you have not paid back or expense that you did not pay in full at the time of purchase. A utility bill for example, is not a debt, but rather a monthly expense. There is no outstanding amount owed once the utility bill is paid. If back payments are owed, then it becomes a debt. Typically a person can sit down and identify 80% to 90% of their debts. Over the next few days, additional debts may come to mind and can added to the list.

Frank and Barbara identified the amount owed. The number at first seemed overwhelming. "How," Barbara thought, "will I ever be able to get out from under this debt? I don't make enough to pay off these debts – and with interest rates and additional needs, the debt just gets bigger and bigger. I am imprisoned by my debt and feel as if I will never get out." She considered bankruptcy in an attempt to free herself from the pressure she felt, but recognized that bankruptcy is taking something from someone, promising to pay for it later and then not making the payment. This is by all definitions stealing. As a Christian, she knows stealing is wrong, and therefore bankruptcy was not an option.

Now committed to removing debt from her life, she spoke with a financial counselor. He shared with her a rule that she should not violate if she was truly interested in gaining the inner solitude of being debt free. If she was truly committed to becoming free from the burden of debt she was to not use her credit cards or incur any new debts during this exercise. Her credit cards must be destroyed, put in a safe deposit box or otherwise removed so she had no access to them. They were to no longer be a part of her life. The purpose for this period of time is for the family to change their spending behaviors. The behaviors that caused the problem of debt needed to be changed. This included the use of credit cards. The focus during this period of time is on frugal living and the removal of debt. With this as the focus, credit cards, even for the sake of convenience are off limits. No exceptions. If a difficult financial emergency occurs, alternative approaches to credit cards must be used. No borrowing for car repairs, clothes, gas, gifts or any other items are allowed. The focus is to become debt free. This is a realistic objective for any family but only if they are truly committed to the process. Evidence of this commitment is a change in spending habits that reflects a lifestyle that spends no more money than is earned each month. Yes, this also requires use of the budget as described in previous chapters. After all, the budget is the pivotal tool on which a healthy stress free financial structure is built. It provides full knowledge of how much is coming in and how much is to be spent in each area.

Take a look at Barbara's list of debts below. Together we will walk through the process Barbara used to free herself from her burden of debt. You can then use this proven system to address the debts in your own life. The approach taken here is simple and straightforward. Your situation may be more complex, but the principles are applicable to any family, even yours, and have been effective in the lives of thousands of families.

Debt Identification		
Debt Name	Amount Owed	Monthly Payment
Sears	$ 150	$ 20
Nordstrom's	$ 300	$ 50
Jack's Furniture	$ 500	$ 100
Dr. Ben Rush	$ 800	$ 100
Discover	$ 1,500	$ 100
Visa	$ 4,000	$ 210
Car	$ 9,500	$ 500
	$	$
TOTAL	$ 16,750	$ 1,080

Once Barbara identified all her debts and ranked them from the lowest total to highest, she transfered the list in that order to the Debt FREEDOM Plan Form that appears at the end of this chapter with one debt written on each form. This process of eliminating debt is called by some, "the snowball plan." We discussed previously how, like snowflakes, small individual savings when combined with other snowflakes can change an entire landscape. If clumped together, these savings, like a large snowball prove to have a much more significant impact if thrown, than a single snowflake would. A snowball will of course start small, but as it combines with additional snow, it grows until it becomes larger and larger and eventually it will become big enough to have terrific force if rolled down a hill. When this principle is applied to debt, the resolution of one debt, when combined with the money from additional debts provides a large bolus of money that, as it grows, can be used to remove all debt. The result is large payments powerful enough to conquer all of a family's financial obligations.

Barbara used this concept and became debt free except for her mortgage in just 15 months. Her mortgage was paid off shortly thereafter. For each expense, starting with her smallest, she filled in a Debt FREEDOM Plan. She listed the debt name, the total amount owed at the time she wrote the plan, the amount of the monthly payment and the "Freedom Date." The Freedom Date is the date she expected the debt to be paid off. Each time a payment was made she wrote in the amount paid and under that she recorded the new amount owed. In this way she could see her debt shrinking.

Debt FREEDOM Plan			
Debt Name	Amount Owed	Scheduled Monthly Payment	Target Freedom Date
_____	_____	_____	___ / ___ / ___
Actual Monthly Payment			
January February March April May June July August September October November December			
$____ $____ $____ $____ $____ $____ $____ $____ $____ $____ $____ $____			
New Amount Owed			
January February March April May June July August September October November December			
$____ $____ $____ $____ $____ $____ $____ $____ $____ $____ $____ $____			

Barbara's smallest debt was to Sears. Monthly, she was making payments of $20. She projected it would take eight months to reach her Freedom Date. However, using the insights she learned in the previous chapter she found "money she never knew she had" by wearing the "snowflake glasses." She was able to identify an additional $130 and she chose to put this money toward debt reduction. This new-found money, added to the $20.00 she was already paying on her Sears bills allowed her to retire the entire bill of $150 in just one month.

Bill #1 Sears
Amount owed: $150
Original monthly payment: $20
New monthly payment: $150
Payoff time for $150: <u>one</u> month

Debt FREEDOM Plan			
Debt Name	Amount Owed	Scheduled Monthly Payment	Target Freedom Date
Sears	$ $150	$ $20	____/____/____

Actual Monthly Payment

January	February	March	April	May	June	July	August
$_150_	$____	$____	$____	$____	$____	$____	$____

New Amount Owed

January	February	March	April	May	June	July	August
$ 0	$____	$____	$____	$____	$____	$____	$____

Barbara was elated when she saw she was able to pay off her first debt so quickly. By adding the money she gained by "finding money she never knew she had" to her smallest debt she was able to eliminate it the first month. This, she decided, deserved a celebration. I agree. **When a debt is retired, a retirement party is appropriate.** This may be a humble celebration, but a celebration is in order. Barbara baked a cake, inflated some balloons, and cranked up the barbeque. People need to celebrate accomplishments and the paying off of a debt is no exception. The first celebration may be much smaller than the final party when the last bill is paid off, but a policy that a debt retirement party of some kind is in order each time a debt is paid off is excellent. It represents a notable achievement.

Once she paid off her first debt, Barbara applied the whole monthly Payment from that debt to the next smallest debt. By adding the $150 she had paid to Sears to the $50 she was already paying to Nordstrom's she was able to pay off that debt also in record time. The payments snowballed as follows:

Bill #2 Nordstrom's
Amount owed: $300
Original monthly payment: $50
New amount available for monthly payment: $200 ($150 Sears +$50 normal payment)
New amount of debt after one month on new plan $250 ($300 original minus the $50 paid last month)
Payoff time for $250: two months

Debt FREEDOM Plan			
Debt Name	Amount Owed	Scheduled Monthly Payment	Target Freedom Date
Nordstrom's	$300	$50	___ / ___ / ___

Actual Monthly Payment

January	February	March	April	May	June	July	August
$ 50	$ 200	$ 200	$___	$___	$___	$___	$___

New Amount Owed

January	February	March	April	May	June	July	August
$ 250	$ 50	$ 0	$___	$___	$___	$___	$___

Adding the $150 she had been paying on the Sears bill to the $50 she had been paying to Nordstrom's provided funds for a monthly payment of $200. At the beginning of February when she was able to apply the money from Sears to her Nordstrom's bill she only owed $250. She was therefore able to retire this debt in two months and it was time again to have a retirement party.

Barbara now had a new problem. In the month of March she had $200 designated toward making a payment and a bill of just $50. What should she do with the extra $150? What a wonderful problem to have. Now, after only three months, she had extra cash. She had several options. One options was to put the money toward the amount she owed on her next largest bill, which was Jack's Furniture. Another was to put the money toward her debt retirement party. This could be a very nice celebration. A third possible use, which has been used by some of my client's is to put this money toward a big reward that will be used once all debts have been paid off. Rewards have included a family vacation, a swimming pool and even a car. Celebrations for good behavior reinforce action and make it easier to continue being frugal and focused on debt resolution.

After the celebration, Barbara added the $200 she had been paying on the Sears and Nordstrom bill to the monthly payment of $100 she had been paying to Jack's Furniture for her vanity table. This provided her with $300 per month to put toward the payment of this debt.

Bill #3 Jack's Furniture
Amount owed: $500
Original monthly payment: $100
New amount available for monthly payment: $300 ($200 from last month +$100 normal payment)
New amount of debt after three months on new plan $200 ($500 original minus the $300 paid over the last three months)
Payoff time for $200: one month

Debt FREEDOM Plan

Debt Name	Amount Owed	Scheduled Monthly Payment	Target Freedom Date
Jack's Furniture	$500	$100	___/___/___

Actual Monthly Payment

January	February	March	April	May	June	July	August
$ 100	$ 100	$ 100	$ 300	$___	$___	$___	$___

New Amount Owed

January	February	March	April	May	June	July	August
$ 400	$ 300	$ 200	$ 0	$___	$___	$___	$___

Barbara was now able to take the $300 she used for payments in April and add it to the $100 she was paying to Dr. Benjamin Rush. This provided her with $400 to pay off this obligation. She had continued to make her monthly payments during the year and in May only owed $400, which she was able to pay off immediately.

Bill #4 Dr. Rush
Amount owed: $800
Original payment: $100
New amount available for monthly payment: $400 ($300 from last month +$100 normal payment)
New amount of debt after four months on new plan $400 ($800 original minus the $400 paid over the last four months).
Payoff time for $400: one month

Debt FREEDOM Plan

Debt Name	Amount Owed	Scheduled Monthly Payment	Target Freedom Date
Dr. Rush	$800	$100	/ /

Actual Monthly Payment

January	February	March	April	May	June	July	August
$ 100	$ 100	$ 100	$ 100	$ 400	$	$	$

New Amount Owed

January	February	March	April	May	June	July	August
$ 700	$ 600	$ 500	$ 400	$ 0	$	$	$

The resolution of the bill to Dr. Rush provided her with a total of $500 to put toward additional debts. She owed $1,000 on her Discover card the beginning of June and was able to use this $500 to pay off the debt in just two months. Once again, a Debt Retirement Celebration was in order.

Bill #5 Discover
Amount owed: $1,500

Original payment: $100
New amount available for monthly payment: $500 ($400 from last month +$100 normal payment)
New amount of debt after five months on new plan $1,000 ($1,500 original minus the $500 paid during each of the last five months)
Payoff time for $1,000: two months

Debt FREEDOM Plan							
Debt Name		Amount Owed			Scheduled Monthly Payment		Target Freedom Date
Discover		$1,500			$100		__/__/__
Actual Monthly Payment							
January	February	March	April	May	June	July	August
$ 100	$ 100	$ 100	$ 100	$ 100	$ 500	$ 500	$_____
New Amount Owed							
January	February	March	April	May	June	July	August
$ 1,400	$ 1,300	$ 1,200	$ 1,100	$ 1,000	$ 500	$ 0	$_____

Barbara and Frank now faced the ominous task of tackling the $4,000 obligation to Visa. Payments were made faithfully and the card had been destroyed, so no new debts occurred. As a result, the debt was now down to just $2,600. Adding the $200 per month obligation to the $500 snowball being used to remove debt they were able to make payments of $700 toward the $2,600 and see it paid off in just four months. The celebration for this was monumental. After all, they had now paid off $7,250 in debt in just eleven months. The stress that had previously permeated their home was nearly resolved. They had peace of mind, knowing how much they should spend for items on their budget and that they would soon be debt free. Important to this process was their commitment to abstain from using their credit in any way until all obligations were paid in full.

Bill #6 Visa
Amount owed: $4,000
Original payment: $200
New amount available for monthly payment: $700 ($500 from last month +$200 normal payment)
New amount of debt after seven months on new plan $2,600 ($4,000 original minus the $200 paid during each of the last seven months)
Payoff time for $2,600: four months

Debt FREEDOM Plan										
Debt Name		Amount Owed		Scheduled Monthly Payment			Target Freedom Date			
Visa		$4,000		$200				/ /		

Actual Monthly Payment

Jan	Feb	March	April	May	June	July	Aug	Sept	Oct	Nov
$ 200	$ 200	$ 200	$ 200	$ 200	$ 200	$ 200	$ 700	$ 700	$ 700	$ 700

New Amount Owed

Jan	Feb	March	April	May	June	July	Aug	Sept	Oct	Nov
$ 3,800	$ 3,600	$ 3,400	$ 3,200	$ 3,000	$ 2,800	$ 2,600	$ 1,900	$ 1,200	$ 500	$ 0

Barbara loved cars. One thing she and Frank agreed on was the decision to drive a luxury automobile. As a result, they found themselves making monthly payments of $500. Beginning in December, they were able to add $700 to their monthly payment and as a result reduce what they owed by $1,200 per month. The car was paid off just four months after they began focusing on this debt.

Bill #7 Car
Amount owed: $9,500
Original payment: $500

New amount available for monthly payment: $1,200 ($700 from last month +$500 normal payment)

New amount of debt after eleven months on new plan $4,000 ($9,500 original minus the $500 paid during each of the last eleven months)

Payoff time for $4,000: four months

Debt FREEDOM Plan								
Debt Name		Amount Owed			Scheduled Monthly Payment		Target Freedom Date	
Car		$16,750			$500		/ /	

Actual Monthly Payment

July	Aug	Sept	Oct	Nov	Dec	Jan	Feb	March
$ 500	$ 500	$ 500	$ 500	$ 500	$ 1,200	$ 1,200	$ 1,200	$ 1,200

New Amount Owed

July	Aug	Sept	Oct	Nov	Dec	Jan	Feb	March
$ 6,000	$ 5,500	$ 5,000	$ 4,500	$ 4,000	$ 2,800	$ 1,600	$ 400	$ 0

The total amount of time needed to pay off $16,750 was just 15 months. This left the $1,200 that was used to pay these debts available to put toward the mortgage. When the $1,200 used for these debts and the $1,500 mortgage payments were combined, they had $2,700 available each month to pay toward the mortgage. If $70,000 were still owed on the mortgage, they would be able to pay off the mortgage and be completely debt free in approximately 26 months. That would leave them with $2,700 each month to put toward retirement, savings, missionary projects, charitable giving, or even purchasing the things they want and need using cash. Not paying interest allows them to use this money for other things as well. Interest from mortgage expense, car payments and credit cards can add up to a significant amount over the period of a year. This money was now available to be used for one another and their children. As Frank so ably stated, "This really is money we never knew we had. We just gave ourselves a raise of $2,700 by paying off the mortgage and other financial obligations. What a boon."

The Avalanche Method

People sometimes comment that the method of starting with the smallest debt and using it as the foundation for paying off additional debts is illogical. After all, money would be better spent if debts with the highest interest rates were paid first. "Why," they ask, "would you pay off a smaller bill with 4% interest before paying a credit card company that charges 25% interest?" This method of paying off the bill with the highest interest first is often called "the avalanche method." After all, once a large obligation with a high interest rate is retired, it comes crashing down making a significant amount of money available to pay many smaller bills. Very disciplined individuals will find this approach attractive.

The snowball method may seem illogical, but it is effective. The reason is the many rewards and reinforcements built into the snowball approach. Every time a debt is paid off, a debt retirement party is celebrated, and the good behavior of focusing on debt payment is reinforced. Conversely, when it takes a long time to pay off the first debt, discouragement sets in. Opportunities to celebrate achievement may take many months. The result is often abandonment of the entire process.

Children can bring life to the snowball approach to debt removal. This is especially true for families who make debt reduction a family project. Frank and Barbara found this to be true. They very candidly brought their family together and explained that they had more debt than they felt was wise. They acknowledged that most of the stress and arguments the family was experiencing resulted from the pressures they felt about spending patterns and the resulting debt. Mom and dad loved one another and their children, and wanted money to be something that enhanced those relationships and not something that pulled the family apart. Together they had decided to bring health to their family relationships and finances and they needed the help of the entire family. For the next year or more, the family was going to focus on how to save money so they could be debt free. Frankie who was 15, Jeremy 10 and Stephanie 6 each responded positively, but with caution. They had seen the negative impact money had on their parent's relationship and family in general. The commitment to building a strong family over getting material possessions or engaging in activities that cost money was attractive to them. A long discussion pursued over the impact this would have upon their lifestyle. Fast food restaurants, designer clothes, soccer lessons, lavish Christmas gifts and expensive vacations were out. Their expectation for what to expect as far as new things was cast, and they were delighted to see mom and dad working closely together on their project and to share in the frequent celebrations.

Frank and Barbara challenged their children to see who could come up with the most ways to save money. Each person was also given a prudent budget for gifts at Christmas, and dining out was no longer an option. They found that by working together toward a mutual goal the family was drawn closer together than ever before.

Having learned about the concept of snowflake glasses they began a contest to see who could come up with ways in which to save even more money that would go toward paying off debt. The children came up with long lists of changes that would provide savings in the family budget. Frank and Barbara were surprised that the children demanded they remain consistent when they wanted to stray even temporarily from their objective. The children continued to be important throughout the debt reduction process. They learned readily that it takes many small decisions to get into debt. It also takes many small wise decisions (snowflakes) to get out of debt. The frequent celebrations for paying off various obligations provided ongoing incentive to the children to "stay the course."

In an effort to show the seriousness of the initiative and that God should be involved with all aspects of a family, the Bridges signed a formal covenant between themselves and with God. The covenant below is similar to the one they used. The family who is truly committed to becoming debt free should read this covenant carefully, discussing its ramifications; and then each person in the family should sign it, signifying they will abide by the agreement.

Lightly printed in the background of the covenant are the words "Jesu Juva." This is the term Johan Sebastian Bach used in the beginning of almost all his pieces of music. These words mean "Jesus, help me." Bach was a phenomenal musician, and, even today, more than three and a quarter centuries since his birth, his music is considered among the finest ever written. By writing these words "Jesus Juva" or the abbreviation "J.J" at the beginning of each piece, he acknowledged that he looked to Jesus to give him the skill and insight needed to complete each composition. How fitting are these words for the family about to embark on the life changing experience of getting out of debt and beginning a debt free lifestyle. The journey will at times seem difficult. Reliance upon Jesus for the strength to remain focused on the long term objective and committing each day to completing the journey will provide added strength. This endeavor requires a change in habits and expectations, things most families will find challenging. Full commitment to freedom from the pressures of debt is expressed by the family willing to sign the covenant and work together toward debt-free status.

Covenant to Achieve Debt Free Status

The undersigned is hereby committed to the successful removal of all debt, to approach debt removal systematically, strategically and to focus attention and priorities on the primary objective of eliminating all financial obligations. This will be done with a prayerful heart, thankful spirit, willingness to sacrifice, problem solve, think creatively, demonstrate self-discipline, and to communicate clearly and non-judgmentally, in order to achieve the desired ends. The eradication of each debt will be celebrated. No new debt will be incurred until all existing debts are paid.

_____   _____
Signature   Signature

_____   _____
Signature   Signature

_____   _____
Signature   Signature

Credit Cards

A quick look at a search engine reveals that people spend between 18% and 35% more when paying with credit cards instead of with cash. (Priya Raghubir at New York University, write in the September issue of the *Journal of Experimental Psychology: Applied and LiveScience* June 2008). Regardless of the percent increase, the principle that people spend more when they use a credit card is one to consider carefully. As one counselee stated, "It hurts less to swipe a credit card than to spend cash." Try it yourself. See if the amount you spend is less when using cash only than when you allow yourself the convenience of using your credit card. Individuals looking to be free from the burden of debt need to remove credit cards from their lives. This may involve a ceremony during which all credit cards are destroyed. The removal of these cards from one's life is a point in time that should be celebrated. Cards can be burned, cut into pieces, placed in a garbage disposal, melted in an oven or dropped in the casket of a deceased loved one. Regardless of the method of removal, the point is that this line of credit is the culprit that has wreaked havoc in the lives of many people. When they make the commitment to get out of debt, they need to change the spending habits that got them into trouble. The only way to get out of debt and to stay out of debt is to cut themselves free from the credit cards that have led them there.

Freedom from credit cards may seem like a difficult task for some. After all, credit cards are so very convenient. On-line purchases require electronic payment. Transactions associated with vacations, business trips and dining out are easily paid for with plastic. Cash is bulky and cumbersome. Keeping records of cash expenditures is more difficult than electronic purchases. Credit cards are convenient but . . . they are not a necessity in Western society today. In fact, they can be easily avoided while retaining many of the benefits they provide. This is done through the combined use of debit cards and cash.

Debit cards provide the convenience of not having to carry cash and provide the ability to make electronic payments. Because the holder of the card can only spend the amount of money they have in their bank account, the card guards against the potential of spending more money than is in the account. It therefore protects the cardholder from racking up credit card bills while at the same time providing electronic records of purchases made. This, combined with the use of cash for regular modest purchase, allows the purchaser better control over spending. With the overuse of credit cards being a growing problem for most families, this combination of debit cards and cash removes the temptation to spend more money than a family has available.

Several years ago, my friend Janets Wecks was sitting at her kitchen table contemplating her financial situation. Janet and her husband Earl, like most families at some point, found themselves with financial difficulties. Credit cards played a major part in this demise. Janet and Earl made some credit purchases as they moved into their new home. They wanted some new furniture as they settled in, and of course the house needed drapes, wallpaper was desired for several rooms, they bought a TV for the family room, a grill so they could enjoy their deck, and of course they saw the need for patio furniture, and a new car to go with their new home. They also wanted to entertain their friends in their new digs and had a great time doing such. In order to get money for the down payment for their new home they spent most of their savings and had little in reserve. Being short on cash, they relied on their credit cards to purchase the things they felt they needed to make their new house "feel like a home." Within several months the card payments revealed they had over extended themselves. Minimal payments became a burden and they found they were not able to pay toward the principle. Their total expenses were larger than the amount of money they brought in each month. The pressure of their debt, coupled with the mentality that they deserve to treat themselves by dining out occasionally, purchase new clothes, and enjoy electronic gadgets such as cable television and cell phones, left them financially compromised. Janet and Earl felt the tension of their finances in their marriage. While they loved their new home, the new level of stress changed the climate of their marriage. Their relationship was not as sweet as before they moved into their new home.

At the end of the year, Janet and Earl looked back over all that had transpired to see what they could learn. One of the lessons they learned was that they spent a great deal of money on interest payments. Janet looked at the amount of money spent on interest by reviewing their year end statements. She asked herself "What could I have bought if I still had that money?" She had spent hundreds of dollars on interest and had nothing to show for it other than the privilege of using the bank's money for her purchases. The realization that essentially, a credit card is a floating loan at 20% or more, left her breathless. She realized that using a line of credit this way is neither frugal nor smart. Had she been patient and waited until she had the money saved for the things she had purchased, she would have been able to acquire many more things because she would not have had to pay the interest. She and Earl would not have felt the same level of tension and pressure that resulted from their debts. The patience of waiting until they had saved enough money to make purchases paid emotional dividends.

In an effort to curb frivolous spending and focus on purchases that are truly needed, she developed a set of guidelines. Before making any purchase she would ask five major questions:

1. Do I need it or do I want it?
2. Is it economically wise?
3. Do I know specifically where the money will come from to pay for it?
4. Are my spouse or accountability partner and I in agreement?
5. Do I have spiritual inner peace about the purchase?

1. Do I _need_ it or do I _want_ it? The difference between these two words is significant. _Needs_ are those things which are required in order to live. They include basic food, shelter, clothing, transportation for work and health care. The quality of these needs as well as most everything else, is _wants_. Needs are necessary for life. Wants include everything else. A family can flourish without having their wants fulfilled.

Distinguishing between needs and wants is sometimes a challenge. When Earl needed shoes for work he purchased well-made safety boots that were breathable, with steel toes, waterproof high-end leather, underfoot cushioning and insulating bottoms. A logger by trade, he needed to protect his feet from uncultivated terrain, falling debris, and the occasional sharp saw. These standards provided safety and protected his health. For $195.00 he considered this an investment in his career. While walking through a high-end department store, Janet spotted a pair of pumps that exactly matched her favorite dress. These were an absolute necessity if she were to look her best. Coincidently, they also cost $195.00. The question the Wecks had to ask themselves was, "Which pair of shoes, if any, are a necessity." Could Earl achieve primarily the same objective for protecting his feet with a pair of shoes that cost $100.00 less? Could Janet find a pair of pumps that provided the same look for $150.00 less? The answer for both was a resounding yes. The need is for foot protection. The want is style and extra features.

Other areas that provided challenges were found in the purchase of groceries, the brand of automobile, gift purchases for others, household appliances, clothing and the purchase of beauty items. Basic questions to consider include: are generic brands of some grocery products just as good or better than name brands? Must Janet wear designer clothes and is it appropriate to drive an expensive car?

2. Is it _economically wise_? Vic and Carolyn Peoples were friends of Earl and Janet. They too were experiencing some tension with their finances, but were considering the possibility of purchasing a swimming pool. Janet and Earl had an open discussion with them about the long-term ramifications of such a purchase. It seemed obvious that keeping the swimming pool full of water would bring additional costs as would the electricity needed to keep the pump running that circulates and filters the water. In addition, Vic was not overly handy and would need to spend $225.00 each spring to have someone remove the cover, prepare the filter and balance the chemistry of the water. In the fall, they would need an additional

$325.00 to have someone replace the cover, clean the filter, blow out the lines and otherwise winterize the pool. Summer months would require a minimum of $10.00 each week for chemicals in addition to the purchase of toys and cleaning equipment. Recognizing the actual cost of the pool, Vic and Carolyn were able to make an informed decision and add these expenses in their budget. They were then able to determine if the purchase was wise for them.

Other purchases that may have obvious hidden costs include clothes that require dry cleaning, the acquisition of a pet (cost for a veterinarian, food and kennel when the family is away), and the purchase of a luxury automobile (maintenance, repair, and fuel). Careful consideration of costs beyond the initial purchase and how these costs fit within the family budget will lead to wiser, much better informed decisions.

3. Do I know specifically *where the money will come from* to pay for it? This question applies to any purchase. Some people are optimistic and tell themselves that one small purchase will not overly impact their overall financial health. This lie is deceptive and is the reason many people are financially compromised. It is the accumulation of many small purchases that are not specifically designated in the budget that create financial crisis. Using the snowflake analogy, the accumulation of many small snowflakes changes the landscape. In the same way, one small non-budgeted item each day of just $5.00 will result in $150.00 in spending over the period of a month and $1,825 over the course of a year. Therefore, if the item is not budgeted or money has not been put away specifically for this purchase, it should not be purchased.

An anticipated bonus, from Aunt Molly's will, money from working overtime or a gift that is yet to be received, do not qualify as spendable income. Only "cash in hand" counts. That is, cash you have actually received, qualifies as money that can be spent. Our friend, Earl, anticipating his usual year-end bonus, used this money before it was received to purchase Christmas gifts. Unknown to him, financial obligations of the company where he worked left the firm without the funds needed to make the usual bonus. Earl had been extra generous, knowing the company was experiencing record sales. He was not aware of the added operational expenses these sales required. The result of his miscalculation left him without the resources needed to pay his bills when they came due in January.

4. Are my spouse or accountability partner and I *in agreement?*
Several years ago, my friend Oliver invited me to view his new woodworking equipment. Having just retired, he purchased the tools for woodworking that he had always wanted. A scroll saw, a radial arm saw, a jig saw, a router, a sander, a planer, a jointer, . . . he beamed as he showed me through his fastidiously organized shop. Everything was in order and he was ready to begin his list of woodworking projects. I asked him what his wife thought of his new toys. "Oh" he said, "she is pretty upset. She wanted to use this money to purchase a trailer so we could travel around together. It appears I may have gained my perfect woodworking shop only to lose my marriage." Oliver's actions appear on the surface to be self-centered. His purchases were made without consulting his wife and collaborating with her on how their money would be spent. He hurt her feelings and damaged their relationship as a result. Had he consulted with her, his decisions may have been much different and the results would have turned out to be more healthy for his total life and marriage.

Insights and input from the people we love and who feel the impact of our purchasing decisions will bring value. They can provide perspectives that would otherwise be missed.

Purchasing decisions made without consulting one's spouse affects the family's budget and can cause serious arguments. Single people and couples who are not confident about certain purchases will find it helpful to discuss major acquisitions with friends or family. Ideally, the best person to discuss this with will be someone with whom you can be candid, will not be judgmental and has a record of providing good insight.

5. Do I have *spiritual inner peace about the purchase*? Sometimes, when considering a purchase, Janet would experience a sense of uneasiness. This was especially true when pressured to make a decision. She learned to listen to her inner voice and postpone buying something when she lacked inner peace. This was not only for large items but for small ones as well. She learned that when she felt an urgency to buy something immediately, it was generally not a wise choice. She asked herself, "What will happen if I do not buy the product today? Will life be significantly better or worse?" Generally, if she missed the sale, or special purchase she would be no worse off than she was at the moment. She learned that few decisions or products are life changing. Failing to take advantage of a sale seldom caused a crisis. If the product was not available or on sale after she took 48 hours to think about it, she was no worse off than before becoming aware of the sale. Focused on living debt free, she would consider the impact of a purchase she felt uneasy about on her ability to continue to reach her financial goals.

Some people insist on using their credit cards. After all, they argue, I'll handle this in a responsible way. The primary guideline for anyone who believes they are in control of their cards is seen in their ability to pay the invoice when it comes in the mail each month. If, at any time, the monthly invoice is not paid completely pay all that is owed each month then abuse has taken place. A credit card is a privilege, not a right. If at any time the monthly invoice is not paid for completely, the rule should be that the holder of the card loses the privilege of using the card until it is paid in full. This protects the holder from falling into the debt trap. The interest paid is not worth the use of the card.

Discussion Questions and Assignments:

1. Barbara Bridge considers bankruptcy to be stealing. What is her rationale? Do you agree? Explain.

2. Credit cards are banned during the process of obtaining "debt free status." Why is this so important?

3. Describe the Debt Freedom Plan Frank and Barbara used to become debt free. What are some of the benefits of using this approach to debt reduction?

4. Use the Debt Identification form to list all of your debts. Describe your emotions as you saw the total amount owed.

5. Complete the Debt Freedom Plan forms for each of your debts. Begin using the system to reduce your outstanding debts. How long will it take for you to become completely debt free?

6. What do you see as your greatest struggle in implementing this system?

7. How much money were you able to save as a result of the exercise of "finding money you never knew you had" that can be delegated to debt reduction? What practical lessons did you learn?

8. What are the advantages of the snowball approach to debt reduction over the avalanche method? Which will work best for you? Explain your rationale.

9. Read the "Covenant to Achieve Debt-Free Status." Why is it important to sign this covenant?

10. Describe the alternative method to using credit cards. How can the avoidance of credit cards make a difference in your life?

11. What are the differences between needs, wants and desires? Explain the impact this can have on a family engaged in the process of becoming debt free.

12. Why is it important for a person's spouse or accountability partner to be in agreement with their purchases?

Debt Freedom Plan

Debt Name   Amount Owed   Scheduled Monthly Payment   Target Freedom Date
_____ / _____ / _____

Actual Monthly Payment

January	February	March	April	May	June	July	August	September	October	November	December
$____	$____	$____	$____	$____	$____	$____	$____	$____	$____	$____	$____

New Amount Owed

January	February	March	April	May	June	July	August	September	October	November	December
$____	$____	$____	$____	$____	$____	$____	$____	$____	$____	$____	$____

Debt Name   Amount Owed   Scheduled Monthly Payment   Target Freedom Date
_____ / _____ / _____

Actual Monthly Payment

January	February	March	April	May	June	July	August	September	October	November	December
$____	$____	$____	$____	$____	$____	$____	$____	$____	$____	$____	$____

New Amount Owed

January	February	March	April	May	June	July	August	September	October	November	December
$____	$____	$____	$____	$____	$____	$____	$____	$____	$____	$____	$____

Debt Name   Amount Owed   Scheduled Monthly Payment   Target Freedom Date
_____ / _____ / _____

Actual Monthly Payment

January	February	March	April	May	June	July	August	September	October	November	December
$____	$____	$____	$____	$____	$____	$____	$____	$____	$____	$____	$____

New Amount Owed

January	February	March	April	May	June	July	August	September	October	November	December
$____	$____	$____	$____	$____	$____	$____	$____	$____	$____	$____	$____

Chapter 8: Doing the Right Things

> Finally, brothers, whatever is true, whatever is noble, whatever is right, whatever is pure, whatever is lovely, whatever is admirable—if anything is excellent or praiseworthy—think about such things.
> (Philippians 4:8, NIV)

When you pray, do you sometimes feel like your prayers hit the ceiling and bounce back to you? Does it seem like they are not leaving the room, let alone getting to God? One of the reasons for this feeling is that we let things interfere with our relationship with God. This relationship is built in part on a spiritual sensitivity, that is, the willingness to listen to God for His guidance and to live as close as possible to the standards He sets. The decisions we make each day, even small seemingly insignificant decisions, have a direct impact upon the closeness or distance that we feel from God. The actions we take, the things we choose to think about, our attitude and our priorities impact how we live out our faith. This in turn influences the depth and scope of our relationship with God and our ability to connect with Him in prayer.

Decisions about our personal finances put us to the test. They show what is most important to us. As we have already seen, priorities determine how we spend our money. If we spend and earn money in ways that please God, we are living out our faith and showing that our relationship with God is a priority. Conversely, if we make choices that are ethically questionable, we demonstrate that our focus is on money or things and not on the Lord.

Money is a wonderful tool when used correctly. It is an instrument that is employed by the church to house its people, establish a worshipful environment and to implement helpful programs. It provides us with a comfortable home to live in, helps educate, feed and clothe our children, and allows for transportation and vacations. But if we love money and things more than we love our Lord, that's not good. Money is beneficial as long as we understand it to be a tool God has given to us to manage for His honor and His glory. As His servants, how appropriate it is to set the highest of standards when spending what He owns.

We all have ethical standards. For Christians, our standards are to be set according to biblical values. Jesus tells us in Matthew 5:48, "Be perfect, therefore, as your heavenly Father is perfect" (NIV). This is the standard toward which we strive. We cannot possibly live up to biblical principles in our own strength; we must therefore look to the Lord daily for guidance. Some people find it easy to use their imperfection as an excuse to compromise ethical standards. They argue that they are still growing in their faith and have not yet reached the point where they have the highest ethics in all things. This is unacceptable. The person who desires a deep personal relationship with Christ will seek to do what is in his best interest at all times. Taking the easy way out of difficult situations is not an option.

Christians are often criticized as being hypocrites. If critics define "hypocrites" as people who do not live up to their own standards, it is a fair assessment. After all, we point to the instructions established in the scriptures as our benchmark. It is impossible to meet this mark one hundred percent of the time. We may not be able to attain perfection, but we should follow the example of the apostle Paul, who said, "Not that I have already . . . been made perfect, but I press on to take hold of that for which Christ Jesus took hold of me" (Philippians 3:12, NIV). Learning to live in a manner that reflects the highest of ethical standards at all times takes more than a lifetime to attain. It requires reliance upon God, sensitivity to His leading, and an understanding of His teachings. What may seem to us to be a minor infraction, a financial "shortcut" that no one cares about, can compromise our relationship with God and taint our witness for Christ. The most important relationship in our life is our relationship with God. We must never do anything that impairs this. It is that relationship that brings value to our life. It must be protected.

We all have reflexes. Some, like a quick pullback from a hot stove, are physical. Others, like our immediate response to ethical decisions, are based not on a physical reaction but on our values. When we find a diamond ring on the table of a secluded conference room or a stack of unattended twenty-dollar bills, our decision as to what to do with that ring or money reveals our core values. If we choose to take the lost item to the "lost and found" so someone can reclaim it, we demonstrate integrity. If we place it in our pocket and later sell the diamond at a pawnshop or spend the money, we again have demonstrated our level of integrity. Small daily decisions like whether we choose to budget money for the church, whether we return borrowed tools, whether we never lie regardless of the circumstances, and whether we allocate the bulk of our budget to the welfare of others such as our spouse and children, impacts our relationship with Christ. The person who desires an intimate prayer life must establish the foundation for this in part by living according to the standards outlined in the scriptures. This includes the instructions outlined in Philippians 4:8 where we are implored to engage in thoughts and deeds that focus on those things that are noble, right, pure, lovely, admirable, excellent and praiseworthy. If our relationship with God is paramount in our life, then the standards of integrity He sets for us must rule our lives.

Let's look at some real life examples of ethical tests that I, and many of the people with whom I have counseled, have faced and determine the financially ethical decisions that should be made:

Taxes
One of my friends, Bob, who is a tax attorney, said, "Many people do not like me to do their taxes because I will not 'fudge' for them. The 'Fudge Factor' should not play a part in their taxes – nor should anything else that has unethical implications. There are many places where we can hide our income or claim expenses we did not incur – but we should not lie." Understating our income, and claiming

deductions that are questionable or fraudulent, can tear at the base of who we are. If we are children of God, then we represent Him. This relationship is at the core of our decisions.

Another friend, Tom, solicited the advice of a tax preparer known for getting excellent results for his clients. Tom followed the advice of this tax preparer, engaging in some decisions that some of us refer to as "creative accounting." Tom was convinced that these questionable decisions designed to saved him money on his return were legal. He admitted they bordered on the edge of questionable interpretation of the law, but he also argued that the government would never audit him. Unfortunately for Tom, just as he was about to make settlement on a new home, he was audited. The tax auditor did not interpret the law with the same level of leniency. He did not grant Tom the benefit of the doubt. The result was a large bill to pay for back taxes, interest on the outstanding taxes, and fines. The size of this bill was significant. He had to dip into the money he and his wife had saved for the down payment and, as a result, were not able to move into their dream home.

We need to make daily decisions that reflect the highest of ethical standards. We should not give ourselves license to make questionable decisions. Instead, we should forego the temptation to give ourselves the benefit of the doubt.

Playing the money game
Several years ago my wife's car broke down on a busy freeway. When the tow truck came, it was driven by a friendly chap who expressed the desire to help us play the money game so the charge to tow the car would not be paid by our family. He indicated the fee was $60.00, but he would give us a receipt for $75.00. Why? He explained that our insurance company would only pay 80% of the bill, so he would write a receipt for $75.00. With this inflated receipt we would be reimbursed 80% of the $75.00, which is the $60.00 we actually paid. He said, this was a service he provided for all his customers. He was "playing the money game" with the insurance company and had found a way to win. With the commotion of the moment, I was not in a position to

pursue an argument. I simply accepted the receipt deciding to think about how to handle what he was proposing later. That evening when I had time to think about what had happened, it was clear that by following through with this transaction I was compromising my standards. To bring closure in the most ethical way possible, I called the insurance company and let them know I had only paid $60.00 and also wrote a note that I attached to the receipt before submitting it to the insurance company. As a result, I received reimbursement for the proper amount. Cheating and lying on this transaction was not worth the impact it would have upon my relationship with God and the respect my wife would have had for me.

Another example of "playing the money game" happened when one of my daughter's playmates hurt herself at school and was taken to the Trauma Unit of the hospital. The receptionist told the family that the insurance would not cover the treatment if it happened at school, so she would indicate on the insurance form that the accident happened at home. The receptionist felt she was being a good citizen by helping this family out with their insurance claim. In reality, she was lying, stealing money from the insurance company, and cheating the family from the satisfaction of knowing they were living ethically.

Money "under the table?"
An acquaintance of mine, Delbert, retired several years ago. In an effort to keep busy and to bring in some added cash, he delivers pizza. His small hourly wage from the modest pizza shop is paid to him in cash, and most of his income comes from tips. He does not declare the money he makes on his taxes, deciding instead to keep it all for himself. According to his rationale "If *I pay taxes on that money, then the government will just take it and spend it on things with which I don't agree are right.*" His wife makes her money providing day care and teaching a dance class. She, too, does all her business in cash, declaring no taxable income.

Collecting tips, providing unlicensed day care in your own home for a fee, earning extra money by providing auto repair, house cleaning services or giving haircuts can serve as a test of ethics and integrity. Any time a person takes cash for a service they perform and fails to report it on their income taxes, he/she is stealing. Stealing in any form, including stealing from the government, is wrong. After all, Jesus himself said in Mark 12:17, "Give to Caesar what is Caesar's and to God what is God's." People who violate this instruction set a poor example for their neighbors and friends and, importantly, for their children. It is likely that such people will feel a barrier between themselves and God when they pray. The reason for this barrier is simple. They have built an obstacle that separates them from God. For the price of a few dollars they have given up the integrity that is fundamental to a healthy relationship with God. They might wonder why the wall exists between them and God when they pray. A little heart searching will reveal that acts of deception may be the culprit. Such acts often become a natural way of life, and Christians take them for granted. We need to proceed through our daily activities giving great thought about how our actions impact our relationship with Christ.

Doing business with people you know to be dishonest

An insurance man came to my friend Phil's house several years ago assuring him he could save Phil's family as much as 25% on his auto insurance. They had a long conversation around the kitchen table. To get the discount, he wanted Phil to lie about several small things. He needed Phil to indicate that one of his cars was for pleasure and that he drove the other car less than ten miles to and from work each day when the commute was actually seventy miles. A ticket received in another state was ignored as was a recent accident. After he showed Phil the money he could save by providing false information, Phil escorted him out of the house. Phil explained to him that his proposal to lie was not acceptable. He was looking to work with an agent who had integrity, and he failed the integrity test. Later, as he and his wife reflected on their time with him, his wife asked, "If he's lying to the company he works for, what's he going to do to us when we have a claim?" Many opportunities come our way in which to reduce costs or to save money. These should, of course, always be explored. However, such opportunities are to be ignored if they require a loss of integrity or compromise our Christian faith.

A common practice among small contractors and subcontractors is dual pricing. Builders, handymen, landscapers and others frequently ask one price if the customer pays by check and another price if the customer pays in cash. The reason for the difference is, again, taxes. If a contractor receives cash payment, there is no record of the transaction, and they will not have to pay taxes. If a payment is made via a check, there is a record of the transaction, and they will have to pay tax. The savings of not having to pay the tax is passed on to the customer. I am not an advocate for higher taxes, but I am an advocate for integrity. If everyone paid the higher price because they knew the reason for the lesser price and wanted to maintain integrity, it would improve the moral fiber of our country. Even if you are personally doing what is right, but know that someone who works for you is acting unethically and you aid in this activity, you have compromised your integrity.

Stealing from your employer
This ethical test is a tough one. Each day millions of people take things from their employer that do not belong to them. Sometimes it is something small such as a pad of paper, a paper clip, a pen or other office supplies. Often it is something much more significant such as productive time. Employers hire people to conduct work during a period of time. Many people use their time at work to do non-work related tasks. They do such things as plan their summer vacation, surf the Internet for information that has nothing to do with their job, prepare for their Bible study or chat with their friends on Facebook or email. When an employer hires an individual to work for them, the employer is entitled to have that person's full attention while they are getting paid. If there is not enough work to be done, the employee should look for additional activities that will be helpful to the company. Each year millions of hours and trillions of dollars are lost because employees steal time from their employer. The standard of

living in our society would increase if we each endeavored to spend all of the time at work focused on the tasks our employer intended.

The cheap compromise – exchanging integrity for pennies?
Soon after he was married, Jason began building a deck on the back of his house. This being his first deck, he asked his father to work with him. In order to space the decking boards accurately, he needed two nails of a certain size (ten-penny) to put between the boards. While at the lumberyard, he found several ten-penny nails on the floor, so he picked two up and put them in his pocket. They were exactly what he needed to do the job. As he was leaving the store and headed toward the car, his father asked him if he remembered to get the two nails. "I have the nails right here he replied."

"I didn't see you pay for them," he said.

Jason said, "I didn't pay for them; they were lying on the floor so I snagged them."

"Oh," he said, "I'm sorry that's all your faith is worth."

Jason's father was pointing out that he had sold out his faith for two ten-penny nails. Jason had considered the items lying on the floor of the store to be waste and of little value. He therefore placed them in his pocket. After all, they were only worth a few cents. The truth is that the owner of the store originally purchased all of the products in his store so he could sell them at a profit and in turn have money to feed his family. Even though the amount of cash was minimal, the principle that we should pay for rather than steal the items we need, is paramount. Jason had sold out the integrity of his faith by stealing two ten-penny nails. It was with little hesitancy that he returned to the store and paid for the nails.

Jason's faith was worth more than a nail and he was not willing to put a wedge between God and himself. It was not a matter of the money –

the store was unlikely to be impacted significantly by a few cents. It was about faith and holding on to biblical standards.

We face ethical tests almost daily. Because we don't always have time to think through our choices carefully, it is important to consider now what moral standards we want to set for ourselves. Are we going to be someone our family and friends see as a person with high moral standards, someone who lives out the foundational principles of their faith, or are we going to compromise our faith for a few dollars?

Traveling on his first business trip to Switzerland, Kevin wanted to explore the city of Basel. He arrived on a Sunday and took a leisurely walk out of the city and into the country. He wandered into Germany, which borders the city, and located a farmers' market. Living in a rural suburb of Philadelphia, he knew farmer's markets well, but this market was different. At the stand, there were all kinds of produce along with a scale. What was unusual was the lack of personnel. This market worked on the honor system. Customers were expected to weigh their vegetables and put money in a bucket once they calculated how much they owed.

The integrity of people in this area truly impressed him. This honor system had been going on for years, with success. As a result, the people who ran that stand were able to be keep their stand open without hiring personnel.

We as Christians need to be trustworthy people known for our integrity. I Thessalonians 5: 21 - 22 implores us to avoid all appearances of evil. It is therefore appropriate, on occasion, to examine our actions with a fresh view, asking ourselves if what we see in our behavior enables us to avoid any appearance of evil? If accused of dishonesty or wrong-doing, would our reputation make such an accusation hard to believe?

In his book, <u>Balancing Life's Demands,</u> Grant Howard outlines what he believes to be the priorities believers should have in order to achieve an optimal level of integrity.

According to Dr. Howard, the main focus of a person's life should be on God. This formulates values and establishes the foundation for all priorities. If an action, behavior or thought in any way violates the instructions and principles outlined in the scriptures, the person will know he is out of bounds. Once a person's focus is on establishing a relationship with God, Dr. Howard explains that the second priority should be on a person's spouse. This will add value to the foundation needed to make wise decisions. Both parties will be able to discuss difficult issues and look to one another for strength. The third area of priority was identified as children. Parents have a high level of obligation to care for their children physically, mentally, psychologically and spiritually. The fourth priority is the individual. At this point, the person is able to focus on their own desires and concerns such as career and hobbies. The decisions we make are based on our priorities. Placing God and others ahead of a person's natural desires sets the stage for wise action.

The true blessings in life come to us when we have our priorities straight; when we seek to do the right things, in the right way, at the right time. The person who looks to the Lord and the instructions He has given in the Scriptures as the foundation for making decisions will have the structure needed to do things right. It will no longer feel as if our prayers bounce off the ceiling. After all, God is with us, guiding our every decision. When we are close with someone we like to be around them, to chat with them about what is important to us, to bounce ideas off them, and to share our own ideas. We are able to anticipate the decisions they would make in a given situation. When God is our partner and confident, we are able to do this with Him. It no longer feels as if our prayers are bouncing off the ceiling. Instead, we are completely transparent with our Lord, sharing our thoughts and seeking His direction as we make financial decisions that impact our life.

Discussion questions:

1. This chapter detailed several "pitfalls" or ethical tests. Comment briefly on each one of the examples in the chapter.

2. How would you characterize your relationship with the Lord? How might the depth of your relationship impact the way in which you make decisions?

3. Describe some of the ethical decisions you have had to make recently. How did you handle the challenges? How could you have improved your response?

4. What might be a good indication that money has come between you and your Lord? Describe some of the steps you can take to remedy this.

5. Consider carefully your priorities in life. Describe the importance of your top three and how they influence the decisions you make in other areas of your life.

6. Consider 1 Timothy 6:10 which reads, "For the love of money is a root of all kinds of evil. It is through this craving that some have wandered away from the faith and pierced themselves with many pangs." How should an understanding of this verse influence the way a person perceives money? Provide some practical examples.

7. Why is the attitude of the heart important in your relationship with God?

8. Read the following verses, and develop a list of the implications for your walk with God.

1 Samuel 16:7
But the Lord said to Samuel, "Do not look on his appearance or on the height of his stature, because I have rejected him. For the Lord sees

not as man sees: man looks on the outward appearance, but the Lord looks on the heart."

Proverbs 4:23
Keep your heart with all vigilance, for from it flow the springs of life.

Proverbs 27:19
As in water face reflects face, so the heart of man reflects the man.

Jeremiah 17:9-10
The heart is deceitful above all things, and desperately sick; who can understand it? "I the Lord search the heart and test the mind, to give every man according to his ways, according to the fruit of his deeds."

Matthew 5:8
"Blessed are the pure in heart, for they shall see God."

Romans 12:1-2
I appeal to you therefore, brothers, by the mercies of God, to present your bodies as a living sacrifice, holy and acceptable to God, which is your spiritual worship. Do not be conformed to this world, but be transformed by the renewal of your mind, that by testing you may discern what is the will of God, what is good and acceptable and perfect.

10. Read the following verses. What insights do they contain for establishing Biblical standards for making financial decisions?

Deuteronomy 8:17-19
Beware lest you say in your heart, 'My power and the might of my hand have gotten me this wealth.' You shall remember the Lord your God, for it is he who gives you power to get wealth, that he may confirm his covenant that he swore to your fathers, as it is this day. And if you forget the Lord your God and go after other gods and serve them and worship them, I solemnly warn you today that you shall surely perish.

Micah 6:8
He has told you, O man, what is good; and what does the Lord require of you but to do justice, and to love kindness, and to walk humbly with your God?

1 Corinthians 10:31
So, whether you eat or drink, or whatever you do, do all to the glory of God.

Chapter 9: The Beauty of Giving

The Christian perspective of how to manage money is based on the understanding that God is the owner of all things. Psalms 24:1 states, *The earth is the LORD's and the fullness thereof, the world and those who dwell therein.* This principle is repeated in 1 Corinthians 10:26 where we find the words, *The earth is the Lord's, and everything in it.* The doctrine that God is the creator and owner of all things has significant ramifications to our perspective of money. If He is the owner, then the way we acquire and spend His resources are to be influenced by what the Scriptures say. After all, the Scriptures are the instructions God has provided to man for how to live.

God has given His people responsibility over the world which He made and which He owns. A passage of Scripture that cannot be ignored is Matthew 25:14-30, known as the parable of the talents, which we discussed in chapter 2. The focus of this parable is that as followers of Christ we are to be wise in how we develop what He has delegated to us. The resources over which we are given control vary from person to person, but the instructions for each one is to follow the general mandates God has given to us. He is the benefactor. We are to follow the principles He has laid out as to how His resources are used.

One of the instructions the Scriptures emphasize is the importance of giving money to the ministry of the Lord. This is something believers have been expected to do since the very beginning of time. Consider Leviticus 27:30-33, from the Pentateuch, which reads:

Every tithe of the land, whether of the seed of the land or of the fruit of the trees, is the LORD's; it is holy to the LORD. If a man wishes to redeem some of his tithe, he shall add a fifth to it. And every tithe of herds and flocks, every tenth animal of all that pass under the herdsman's staff, shall be holy to the LORD. One shall not differentiate between good or bad, neither shall he make a substitute for it; and if he does substitute for it, then both it and the substitute shall be holy; it shall not be redeemed. (ESV)

This passage is very specific. Of all that God has given to His people, He requires one tenth be designated directly to His ministry. If He gives someone ten things, He wants one of those ten things to go directly to His work. If someone is not giving one-tenth of what they have received, they are being disobedient to God. Note how the importance of this act is emphasized by the demand for a penalty payment if the tithe is not paid in a timely manner. He said, "If a man wishes to redeem his tithe" – that is, keep it for himself – "he shall add a fifth to it." God is requiring 20% interest on any tithe that is not given directly, and in a timely manner, to the work of the Lord. The implication here is that believers, who have not been tithing up to this point, owe their unpaid tithe, plus the 20% interest.

This passage also says we should not differentiate between the good and the bad. People who experience a very prosperous year need to give a minimum of one tenth of their wealth to the work of the Lord. If they have a less than good year financially, it is still a tenth.

Meeting with a group of deacons over coffee several years ago, we began discussing the question, "Is it 10% of our gross income or our income after taxes." We found that the concept of giving one's tenth of income, before taxes or other expenses, is introduced among other places in the book of Proverbs. Special note can be made that Proverbs is found in the section of Scripture referred to as "Wisdom Literature." People who study wisdom literature do so in order to learn the principles that lead to wisdom. Note the emphasis on the words "first fruits." In Proverbs 3:9,10 (ESV), it states

Honor the LORD with your wealth and with the "first fruits" of all your produce; then your barns will be filled with plenty, and your vats will be bursting with wine.

Our question under discussion was "What are the "first fruits?" I would argue that for us, first fruits are our initial income. That is before taxes and other expenses, not after taxes. It is the very first money that comes into our possession. Qualifications for exemptions are not listed in the scriptures. If your salary is $1,000 a week, then it is easy to determine that the amount to be tithed is $100. After taxes, a person's paycheck may be only $720, but that is not a part of the equation. The Lord has asked for 10% of the initial amount.

This money is to be designated to support the ministry of God. In the Old Testament, as today, it was difficult for people to spend time gaining a livelihood and, at the same time, carry out the complete work of the ministry. Professionals are needed to study the Scriptures in order to help us learn from them and to carry out many of the ministry related tasks that are part of the church. To resolve this issue, the Lord designated the Tribe of Levi to carry out this responsibility for the other eleven tribes. In Deuteronomy 18:3-5 we find the instructions for the eleven tribes in which they are directed to take care of the physical needs of the tribe of Levi.

And this shall be the priests' due from the people, from those offering a sacrifice, whether an ox or a sheep . . . The first fruits of your grain, of your wine and of your soil, and the first fleece of your sheep you shall give him. For the LORD your God has chosen him out of all your tribes to stand and minister in the name of the LORD, him and his sons for all time. (ESV)

Some people argue that the money given to the priests was also used to manage the government of the people. Israel was after all a Theocracy. While this is true, later when under the rule of other countries, Israel was still expected to tithe even when paying taxes to countries that had conquered them. The priests, called to serve, are to be taken care of by those whom they were called to serve. Again, in Nehemiah 10:39 (ESV), we find direct instructions that state,

For the people of Israel and the sons of Levi shall bring the contribution of grain, wine, and oil to the chambers, where the vessels of the sanctuary are, as well as the priests who minister, and the gatekeepers and the singers. <u>We will not neglect the house of our God</u>. (emphasis mine)

When believers do their part, it affects in a most positive way the work of the Lord. Depending on the survey, it is estimated that the average family who regularly attends a conservative, evangelical church, gives between 2.7% and 3.5% of his or her income to the work of the Lord. That is, of course, far less than 10%! Imagine if every believer did in fact give the full 10%. What would happen if the local church, mission agencies, and parachurch organizations such as InFaith had three-times more money to work with than they have today? The impact upon the nation and the world would be significant.

I work for America's oldest home mission society. InFaith traces its roots back to ministry that started in 1790. The people to whom we minister are those who would otherwise be unreached with the gospel message by the traditional church. The organization has therefore complimented the work of the local congregation and denominations in the United States for over 200 years. Thousands of churches have been started in the past century alone by the work of InFaith missionaries to America. Each missionary couple must raise the money they need so they can carry out their ministry. Some people who are very effective in ministry find it a struggle to raise funds they need to engage in the work to which they feel a divine call. How nice it would be if three times more money was available for ministry because believers throughout America were giving the amount requested of them in the Scriptures. If this were the case, and finances were not such a stressful issue, we would be able to send out more missionaries. A full tithe or more by everyone would also empower local congregations to have the programs, staff and equipment they need in order to minister in more creative ways to larger numbers of people.

Unfortunately, Satan is crafty and knows how people think. He has been around for thousands of years and has invested the time and attention needed to learn the art of manipulation. Together, with his army of well-trained fallen angels, he is able to use this knowledge to influence our priorities. Instead of following what we know to be right, we sometimes listen to the ungodly messages placed in our ears. We hear such messages as, "You're just one person. The small amount you contribute won't make that great an impact," or "You need the cash for bills right now. Hold off for a few months until you get your finances under control," or "You are a child of God, a prince(s). The Lord wants you to have nice things while you are here on earth, not just in heaven. How can you have things and live the way God intends for his children if you give your money away to the church?" The result of influencing us one by one makes the ministry of the church much less effective because of a lack of resources. It is just like those snowflakes we discussed in previous chapters. One by one they accumulate, until they cover the ground, and ultimately change the landscape. So the impact of individuals, cutting back one by one and giving only a third of what they should, makes a difference in the work of the Lord. Conversely, if one by one each believer would give the full tenth of their income or more, the spiritual and moral landscape of our nation would change.

People should of course pray for a spiritual revival in our nation. How much more fruitful their prayers are when they know they have done their part by empowering missions and churches by giving financially. The Scriptures are very pointed when addressing this issue. Keeping money designated to the work of the Lord to use for one's self is described as stealing from God. This is more than just being disobedient. It is theft. Malachi 3: 8-10 states:

Will a man rob God? Yet you are robbing me. But you say, 'How have we robbed you?' In your tithes and contributions. You are cursed with a curse, for you are robbing me, the whole nation of you. Bring the full tithe into the storehouse, that there may be food in my house. And thereby put me to the test, says the LORD of hosts, if I will not open the windows of heaven for you and pour down for you a blessing until there is no more need. (ESV)

Do note, as in many Scriptures, we find in this passage a curse from God when we disobey, and blessings if we do obey. And how does He bless us? As we examine life, we find that the blessings that are most valuable to people are not generally things. Rather, the joy we receive in life is found in relationships, events, time with family and friends, experiences in church, school, vacation and work. God does not always bless us just with *possessions* but also with the *things that really matter*. People who give financially do so because they have assessed their priorities, focusing attention on what truly important, that bring obedience to God. When God is at the forefront of our priorities, everything else takes a new perspective. What we value at that point are those things which are right, pure and good. These things tend to bring peace and happiness. Greed, possessiveness, and success, sometimes at the demise of others, are no longer a part of our thinking. The result is an inner peace that many in this world find difficult to achieve.

Part of the reason it is hard to tithe has to do with what is valued in our society. For most in our culture, personal worth is in the things they possess. This includes the house in which they live, the kind of car they drive, the style and make of the clothes they wear, the quality of schools their children attend, and the kind of vacation they take. When they give to the Lord, they're taking money from the things that society says is of value, and putting it towards something that's not tangible. There is little to show in a physical way for where the money has gone. Mature believers understand that what is of greatest value is not what we possess; rather it is a relationship with God. We learn, as Dr. Sinclair Ferguson so clearly stated, "Christ minus everything is still everything, and everything minus Christ is at the end of the day absolutely nothing." (Sermon at Tenth Presbyterian Church November 7, 2010). Giving to the work of the Lord breaks the control of money over our lives. It helps us recognize that it is our relationship with Christ, not the possession of things, that is of greatest value.

The importance of maintaining priorities that center on spiritual things is emphasized throughout the Scriptures. Matthew 6:19-21 builds on this theme, quoting Christ as saying; *Do not lay up for yourselves treasures on earth, where moth and rust destroy and where thieves break in and steal, but lay up for yourselves treasures in heaven, where neither moth nor rust destroys and where thieves do not break in and steal. For where your treasure is, there your heart will be also.* (ESV, emphasis mine)

Highlighted here is the need to place value in areas that should be important to us. Where we put our money, attention and time is a reflection of what is of value to us. When we examine our bank statement, checkbook, and credit card statements, we learn where we have placed an emphasis. Balance is healthy, and this should be revealed in our finances. Part of this balance is the designation of funds to the work of the Lord due to our love and allegiance to him.

Some people look at the Scriptures about tithing listed above and observe that the verses which direct a tithe are all from the Old Testament. I have heard people say, "These are all verses from the law. Today, we live under grace and are no longer bound to follow these rules." Christ addressed this issue when, in Matthew 23:23, he stated,

Woe to you, scribes and Pharisees, hypocrites! For you tithe mint and dill and cumin, and have neglected the weightier matters of the law: justice and mercy and faithfulness. These you ought to have done, without neglecting the others. (ESV)

In this passage he was commending the Pharisees for following the law by tithing even the most insignificant spices. At the same time, he condemned them for failing to follow the overall theme of Scripture. His instruction was to tithe ("These you should have done") without forgetting to follow the character traits reflected in justice, mercy and faithfulness to God. Tithing is a part of the overall instructions we receive that sets us up for a healthy relationship with God. Those who argue that Christ's instructions are not valid for believers today, because the Pharisees were under the law, would also need to negate all of his other teachings. After all, everyone in Israel whom he taught was at that time under the law.

The Scriptures are full of instructions designed to help us with our faith. Our responsibility is to be obedient to Him out of love and respect for Him even when we have not gained the level of maturity to understand why the mandate is important. Let me illustrate. When my son Kevin was a little boy, he loved to play soccer. He would kick the soccer ball back and forth across the yard and against the garage door. We had a standing rule. If the ball went into the street, he was not allowed to run into the street to retrieve it. He was to call an adult and have them get it for him. Soon after we moved into a new neighborhood, he kicked the ball against the garage door and it ricocheted past him and rolled out into the street. He took a stick and reached out as far as he could, but he couldn't reach it. Kevin looked around and did not see his mother or me so he quickly ran into the street to pick up his ball. Unfortunate for him, I was watching from inside the house and called him inside where he was punished. For us, punishment generally consisted of sitting on a step without anything to do except to think about what was done wrong. I was not interested in hearing an excuse about why Kevin had broken the rule or to have a discussion about how unfair he felt the rule to be. My desire was that he be safe. The risk that he might be struck by a car was real and the potential consequences of such an event was greater than what was acceptable. My love for my son was strong and his safety paramount. The reason for the rule was to protect his life, and as a parent, it was my responsibility to enforce it. His approval and understanding as a seven-year-old was not part of the equation. He was to follow the rule. His understanding and approval was secondary. God loves us with a greater capacity than we can imagine. He too has provided for us rules to protect us and to enrich our lives. Our job is not always to fully understand or approve His instruction for us. Our mandate is to be obedient to His instructions.

Obedience is not without qualification. Not only are we to do what our Lord requires of us we should do it out of love for Him and with a cheerful heart. In 2 Corinthians 9: 6-8 we find,

The point is this: whoever sows sparingly will also reap sparingly, and whoever sows bountifully will also reap bountifully. Each one must give as he has decided in his heart, not reluctantly or under compulsion, for God loves a cheerful giver. And God is able to make all grace abound to you, so that having all sufficiency in all things at all times, you may abound in every good work. (ESV, emphasis mine)

This passage does not mean that we are exempt from giving until we can be cheerful about our obedience. What it is saying is that we need to work at gaining the level of spiritual maturity in which we are cheerful about delegating to the work of the Lord, that which He has required from us. Obedience, even if the act is not fully understood or we do not agree with the mandate, is greatly pleasing to God, when done cheerfully out of love. Our cheerful heart is something He has told us He specifically loves.

When my daughter Kerri was just a little girl, her brother and mother went out of town for the day to participate in a soccer tournament. That left Kerri and me alone. When lunchtime came, I realized she needed something to eat. I took out some bread (which I had purchased previously), and put some peanut butter (which I had purchased) on one side and jelly (which I had purchased) on another slice. I put the two slices of bread together and cut them into four sections. Placing them on a plate I gave the sandwich to her to eat. The question is, "Who owned that sandwich?" The answer, of course, is that I owned the sandwich but had given it to her to eat. I owned the bread, I owned the peanut butter, I owned the jam and in a legal sense, I even owned her. But I gave the sandwich to her to eat because I loved her and wanted her to be nourished and to eat something she enjoyed. Soon after beginning to eat, she realized I had not made anything for myself and she asked, "Daddy, would you like to have part of my sandwich?" Her heart was not on herself alone. She did not selfishly demand she retain the entire sandwich for herself. Instead, she was thinking about me and desired to give to me something over which she had been given control. What she offered to me after receiving the sandwich was delightful. It was pleasing to know that she loved me enough to want to give something to me. This made me think about how pleased the Lord must be when we cheerfully give tithes and offerings to Him, because we love Him. It is true that He asks us to designate gifts and offerings. What He is looking at when we give is both our obedience and our attitude. A cheerful attitude, when it comes to giving to our Lord, is what He desires and appreciates.

Not everyone has grown in their spiritual walk to the point in which giving is something they enjoy. Such people need to begin their quest out of obedience with the desire to grow in spiritual depth and love for God, so that giving is something they do cheerfully because of their love for their Lord.

Troy and Andrea decided they wanted to start tithing. Living on an already austere budget, they struggled with how this would impact their life together. Immediately cutting ten percent from their gross income seemed daunting. Troy, being very practical, established a systematic approach to reach their goal. He decided to phase in giving over a period of time. Starting small, Troy and Andrea began giving 2% of their income for six months. This provided them with the pleasure of giving without creating a devastating impact on their budget. At the end of six months they added an additional 2% and six months later another 2%. In this way they were able to adjust their spending habits to accommodate their desire to give as their Lord commanded. In just 2½ years, this family was tithing at the appropriate level. The amount they gave did not stop there. Recognizing they had not been tithing for a number of years, they determined to exceed ten percent to help make up for the funds they had missed in the past, and because they wanted to give to the work of the Lord to show their gratitude to Him. They recognized ten percent is just a basic requirement. Gifts above this will bring added spiritual rewards. A good rule of thumb I give to people first developing their financial plan is what is called the 10-10-80 rule. This rule dictates that 10% of a family's gross income (before taxes) goes to the Lord's work, 10% goes to savings and they live on what is left. This makes for a healthy balance. One of my colleagues, when sharing this concept with me, explained that he and his wife have used this for over 30 years. It has provided for them the discipline needed to establish right priorities, to remain focused on their allegiance to God, and to have sufficient funds set aside for unexpected bills, vacations and retirement. This 10-10-80 rule allowed them a sound financial base. As a result, they felt secure financially. The scriptures ask us to excel in all we do. 2 Corinthians 8:7 provides instruction about the level of giving. It states,

But as you <u>*excel in everything*</u> *– in faith, in speech, in knowledge, in all earnestness, and in our love for you – see that you excel in this act of grace also.* (ESV, emphasis mine)

What does excellence in giving mean? Each person will need to determine what this means to them personally, but it does indicate that giving should be far more than ten percent.

There are things that can be done that will make giving a more enjoyable experience. My father, a missionary in Oregon, started a number of churches. He was keenly aware of the financial challenges of ministries throughout the state. Sometimes ministries or individuals had specific needs, and he wanted to be able to step in and help. He created what we called the Bartruff Family Giving Fund. This was a special bank account where my parents, my sister, her husband and I would pool our money for ministry. We were already giving to the church and to certain missionaries individually, and in addition we put extra money into this account. The account grew monthly and was intended specifically for special projects. On one occasion, a camp in central Oregon needed funds to re-roof cabins. As a family, we discussed the needed and designated funds to this project. On another occasion, a family was falling apart because the father was out of work, their three girls and one boy needed clothes for school, and their rent was due. Health issues were also a part of the scenario. Our family was able to assist the family financially, while my father helped them put their affairs in order so that in subsequent months they did not have to rely on the generosity of others. Other projects included assisting churches with building projects, purchasing craft materials for Vacation Bible School programs and printing literature to be used primarily by the missionaries who worked with my father. It was fun to have our own giving fund and to look for ways in which our family could make a difference. Some people use this concept to help in other ways. Each year my home church sponsors 90 to 160 teenagers who take short-term mission trips to ghetto neighborhoods in the Philadelphia area and abroad.. The experience is life changing for the teenagers as they share the gospel message with others. Members of our congregation set money aside during the year so they can contribute to this project each spring. The church gains a sense of vigor as we send these students off to minister during the summer months. For our family and our church, giving is something that draws us together as a stronger unit and encourages us in our faith.

The scriptures teach that giving should be done logically and systematically. 1 Corinthians 16:2 teaches:

On the first day of every week, each of you is to put something aside and store it up, as he may prosper, so that there will be no collecting when I come. (ESV)

This instruction was given by the Apostle Paul to the church in Corinth, so as a church body they would be prepared to give missionary gifts. We learn from this the value of systematic giving. The family who receives monthly paychecks, but waits until December to give their tithe for the year, will typically find giving in December to be a tremendous challenge. But giving as soon as the money comes in takes much less effort. The weekly setting aside of money we have budgeted to be used directly for the work of the Lord helps us stay on task.

Some people ask where to delegate their funds. Should it all go to their church? Should the bulk go to mission organizations? How much should be given to special missionary or outreach projects? Designating money should be done prayerfully and with careful thinking. Family discussion over how much should go to various causes allows each person to recognize the influence they can have in a variety of ways. The Giving Plan provided on page 164 is designed to help with this. Once the amount of the tithe and gifts are determined, specific amounts can be targeted to various organizations, including the local church, on a monthly basis. It is a spiritually encouraging exercise for a family to sit together and talk about what Christian organizations should be targeted, as well as future projects. Completing and periodically reviewing this Giving Plan allows everyone in the family to be aware that yes, your family, through obedience to God, is making a difference in the world, and that the Lord will be glorified through your cheerful obedience.

Giving Plan

For the_____**family**

10% of Total Income $_____

Organization	Monthly Amount	Annual Amount
_____	$_____	$_____
_____	$_____	$_____
_____	$_____	$_____
_____	$_____	$_____
_____	$_____	$_____
_____	$_____	$_____
_____	$_____	$_____
_____	$_____	$_____
_____	$_____	$_____
_____	$_____	$_____
_____	$_____	$_____
Total	$_____	$_____

Potential Future Designations

_____	$_____	$_____
_____	$_____	$_____
_____	$_____	$_____

Discussion Questions and Assignments:

1. Based on your understanding of the Scriptures, is it important for Christians to give some of their income to the work of the Lord? What percentage do you believe this to be? Explain your rationale.

2. Who is the owner of all things? What has the Lord used as an instruction book to indicate how He would like His possessions managed? Do you feel obligated to follow His directive? Explain.

3. Should a Christian use his gross income or his net income (after taxes) to base his minimal level of giving to the work of the Lord. Describe your rationale.

4. Some people do not believe they are living under the law of the Old Testament Scriptures and are therefore not obligated to give to the work of the Lord. Provide an explanation for why giving is important today referring to Matthew 23:23 in your response.

5. How might the spiritual and ethical standards in our country be different if every believer gave a minimum of ten percent of their income to the work of the Lord?

6. Comment on the words of Dr. Sinclair Ferguson, "Christ minus everything is still everything, and everything minus Christ is at the end of the day absolutely nothing." What impact might this statement have on a person's approach to life and giving to the work of the Lord?

7. How does giving to the work of the Lord break the control of money over our life?

8. 2 Corinthians 9:6-8 says, "God loves a cheerful giver." What responsibility does that put on the believer? How might this be a formidable spiritual challenge?

9. Giving a minimum of ten percent of a person's gross income can be daunting to an already strained budget. How might a family work into the system gradually? Is a gradual implementation of giving acceptable or must it come all at once? Explain your reasoning.

10. How would excellence in giving be displayed in your life? Use the Giving Plan form provided to show how you would like to designate funds to ministry.

Chapter 10: So You Want to be a Millionaire

We have explored in this book how to set God centered priorities, how to communicate about money, establish ethical standards, develop a financial plan, how to get out of debt, and about the beauty of giving to others. Now that we are on track with the fundamentals, we can explore the steps needed to acquire the level of wealth needed to be financially independent. Most people find an adequate level of wealth is one that provides a sufficient flow of cash so they are able to pay their current monthly bills. But this does not leave them with the peace of mind that comes to those who build the level of wealth that leaves them financially secure during even the most difficult of financial circumstances.

The Scriptures advocate a perspective of finances that provides such peace of mind. Proverbs 21:20 states, "In the house of the wise are stores of choice food and oil, but a foolish man devours all he has." Money put aside for the future provides a sense of financial security. According to this verse, such action reflects wisdom. Unfortunately, many people spend all they bring in and sometimes even more. They are not prepared for the inevitable emergencies that are a natural part of life.

My friend Jeff is a good example. He owns two jet skies, two motor boats, two cars, a truck, a vacation home at the Maryland shore (actually a trailer with a deck), a golf cart, and a trailer for his pickup. He also has four cell phones on his account and cable service at both his home in the city and at the shore. Jeff brags about the wonderful deals he made when buying these toys, justifying their purchase. He also complains that he does not have money to invest for retirement or as a safety net if an emergency were to arise. When his truck broke down it created a financial crisis. Spending his money on toys today has removed the possibility that he will be able to take care of himself and his wife if they have a financial or medical crisis, and nothing is set aside for when they reach the age at which they will need to stop working. Jeff jokes that the future will take care of itself, and he plans to work until he drops. Unfortunately for Jeff and his wife, the future will come and he has failed to face the demise his priorities have set for him and his wife.

Like Jeff, most Americans spend all they earn as soon as it comes in and soon find themselves deeply in debt. Money needed for emergencies, vacations, home improvements, health expenses and even retirement become a burden that drags them down. Time after time people tell me "I don't have enough money to save let alone invest," or "I spend what I need during the month, and whatever is left at the end, that's what I save – which is seldom anything." They do not understand the basic concepts that separate the rich from the poor. People who have learned to live on a budget and live within their means, no matter their income, have learned to designate significant savings and investment in their budget so they have the structure to seriously contribute funds each month, quarterly or yearly. It is for this reason that the Budget Worksheet in chapter three lists savings as the first budgetary item.

Recently, I was watching a television show that focused on personal finance. A man from Australia called in with his finance question. He indicated he would like to own a house but did not have enough money to make a down payment. As the conversation ensued, he shared that his annual income was $450,000. The reason he did not have enough money for a down payment was that he lived for the moment instead of opting for balance in his life. If there was a concert in London that he wanted to see, he would hop on a plane and fly to London. He spent the month of August on vacation at a wonderful resort in France. He wore expensive clothes. In fact, one of his suits alone cost several thousands of dollars. Because he was living an extravagant lifestyle, he was unable to save money for a house of his own. Did he have the resources? Of course he did. If he truly desired to become a homeowner, he needed to evaluate how he was spending his money and make adjustments so he could reach this objective. Savings needed to be a priority item in his budget.

You may not make $450,000 a year, but it's likely that your income has increased during your career. It's also likely that it isn't any easier for you to save with a higher income than it was with a lower one. A frequent observation made by financial counselors is that, "Spending expands to meet any added income." This is why savings must be a priority in any and every budget. No budget is complete without this item. The downward spiral of debt will not go away unless money is set aside from which to draw in an emergency. Credit card debt will continue to grow if people look to it to supplement their cash flow instead of reaching into savings for unexpected or atypical expenses. It is for this reason that everyone, including individuals with substantial debt, should put some money into savings each month. Not only does it provide a buffer and resources for the future, it activates a change in mindset. Instead of living under the cloud of debt, spending irresponsibly, and reaching for the credit card when a financial need arises, saving demands self-discipline, provides hope and gives a sense of control over the future.

The recommended amount of savings for the average family is to follow the 10-10-80 rule. With this rule, 10% of each paycheck goes toward savings, 10% goes directly to the work for the Lord and 80% is then spent on living expenses. This is not a great amount of money for people with a lifestyle that fits within their income, but some people, as they begin to address this aspect of their financial plan, find this formula overwhelming. Such people can begin the process of saving by systemically putting a small amount away each paycheck and increasing the amount over time. Some find it challenging to put away as little as $20 per paycheck, but this is an exercise they must begin if they are to have a financially healthy future.

The first goal in establishing a healthy savings plan is to set a target of having $1,000 in savings that is easily accessible to cover emergencies. With this amount in hand, small emergencies such as auto repairs or the need for new appliances can be paid for with cash. The need to reach for the credit card and the debt and interest rate it represents are eliminated.

The second goal is to have at least three months' spendable income hidden away for emergencies. That is, the amount of money the family would need in order to pay its bills if no money were to come in to the household for three months. This provides a cushion large enough to avoid a financial catastrophe if family wage earners lose their source of income or there is a large unexpected expense. The need for a new roof or to pay medical expenses can wreak havoc on a family financially.

Some financial experts use the phrase "pay yourself first" to describe the process of designating money to be put in savings before budgeting for any other expense. You are taking care of yourself first by establishing funds for yourself so you have money from which to draw, so that you will not have to borrow on your credit card thereby pulling yourself deeper into debt.

Financial Independence
Financial independence is a noble objective. Each person must determine the standard of living that is right for their situation, but becoming financially free and not held down by the requirement of employment provides a great sense of accomplishment. There are several steps that go into the process of gaining financial independence. The first of these steps is to develop a realistic budget. Considerable time has been spent in previous chapters addressing the many nuances in developing such. Once this is established, the second step which is to get out of debt must be addressed. Debt is a disease that infects a budget, putting a reasonable lifestyle and planning for the future at risk. This we have also addressed.

The third step is to become your own banker. Sounds attractive, does it not? Yes, I am suggesting that you should become the owner of your own bank (or a bank account that you own and serves as your own personal bank). Think for a moment about what a bank is. Is it not a place where people put their money, collect interest and, when they need money they go to the bank and retrieve or borrow funds? You can gain all the benefits of being a banker by putting money each month into a savings account (your own stash of money) until you reach your first goal of $1,000 and second goal of three months spendable income, and then borrowing from this account (your bank) each time money is needed for an emergency or atypical expense. You will of course need to pay yourself back once any money is borrowed, but how much sweeter it is to pay yourself back then to pay a commercial bank or the holder of your credit card.

The next time your washer or dryer needs to be replaced, you won't need to use your credit card to make the purchase and then pay the holder of your credit card interest. Instead, you can borrow from yourself, buy the washer with cash, and pay yourself back. The money you have in your savings bank earns interest. If you earn 3% on your savings and avoid paying 17% on a credit card loan, you come out ahead by 20%. Some of my more creative friends give their personal bank (bank account) a name such as George's Bank, or The Smith Bank or Janet's Savings Bank. Regardless of your level of creative spin, the principle behind the concept of becoming your own banker provides sound financial health, decreases family stress, and sets the stage for additional savings and investing. This includes putting money away for vacations, special trips, Christmas presents, purchasing an automobile or for home improvements.

I am often asked when should a family who has substantial debt begin investing. The answer is "now." Money needs to be placed into the bank for emergencies. Systematically placing some money in savings for this purpose protects the family from future disasters. It also establishes healthy behavior patterns. Typically, families will never have money for savings or investments if they do not begin allocating some savings in their budget even when they are engaged in serious steps toward debt reduction.

Once you have met your savings goals of three months living expenses in savings, it is time to invest for the future. This includes the process of systematically investing for retirement and also gaining wealth.

The fourth step is to invest for the future. Everyone has the ability to achieve financial freedom. All that is required is to consistently put away funds each month in an account that provides reasonable return on investment, and of course, time plays an important role. Consider, for example, the couple that determines that in order to retire they need a million dollars. This is a less than challenging task which they can achieve easily given consistent savings over a period of time.

Provided at the end of this chapter is what is identified as a Compounding Chart. Imagine for example you are 25 years old and desire to have $1,000,000 so you can retire in 40 years at the age of 65. All you need to do is to run your finger down the left hand column until you get to the number 40. You will then move your finger over to the 10% column where you will find the number (factor) 442.59. You will have chosen 10% because you know that the stock market grew an average of 9.6% between 1926 and 2008. You feel comfortable that you will be able to average approximately 10% on your investments during the next 40 years. This number 442.59 is the figure you will use to divide into $1,000,000 to learn the amount to invest annually in order to meet your objective. In this case, $1,000,000 divided by 442.59 equals $2,259.43. The person who invests $2,259.43 per year for 40 years will have a nest egg of $1,000.000. Divided by twelve months that translates into $188.30 per month or $6.45 per day. We are talking about concepts in this illustration, and there are several variables that need to be considered. Notably, the compounding nature of multiplication will actually require slightly less per month. We are also not able to guarantee 10% per year for each of the next 40 years. Some years will provide considerably less return on investment and other years will provide considerably more. Regardless of the actual returns, the person who consistently puts $188.30 away each month for 40 years in the stock market will have considerable funds if the market mirrors its performance during the past 80 years.

The individual who is not willing to wait 40 years and is interested in securing $1,000,000 in just 20 years needs only to follow the same formula for determining how much to put away each month. First, they will run their finger down the year column to the year 20. You will then move it over to the 10% column where you will find the number 57.275. This is the number to use to divide into $1,000,000 to learn the amount needed to invest annually in order to meet your objective. In this case $1,000,000 divided by 57.275 equals $17,459.62. This means your investment annually of $17,459.62 or $1,454.96 each month over a 20-year period will provide you with a nest egg of $1,000,000.

Some people are more conservative and not willing to invest in instruments that mirror the stock market. They can use this chart using the variables of the number of years over which they wish to invest and the anticipated interest rate to determine the amount of return they can expect. The amount of return expected may be 8%, 5%, or even 3%.

Some people may believe they do not need a million dollars when they retire. Half of that amount or ½ million dollars will require $3,039.70 per year, $252.30 per month or just $8.33 per day in just 30 years. Most people can find ways to adjust their spending to secure $8.33 per day. This is significantly less than one hour's work each day for most people. We spent an entire chapter addressing ways in which to find money we never knew we had. There is little excuse for people who understand this concept to not put away sufficient funds so they are able to be secure in the future.

You may find it best to start with a small dollar amount or percentage of your income and increase the amount over time. An initial monthly investment of 2% into a mutual fund with the goal of adding 2% each year to the savings or investing line in the budget for the next four years, will result in an investment of 10% of income. The gradual progression of adding just 2% each year will have minimal impact on spending. Had you begun this process five years ago, you would have achieved your goal today. My friend David Thompson reports that he contributes 50% of his raise in wages each year to investments. In this way, he has achieved his objective in just four years. According to David, the gradual progress of this process has provided little pain and significant satisfaction. Stepping back and looking at financial objectives over the long-term provides the opportunity to develop and implement a strategy that will provide the desired end results.

In the same way the snowball principle removed debt in chapter seven, it also provides the money needed to build wealth for the future. A common statement made by investment counselors is, "Money makes money and the money that money makes, makes money." Understanding this concept can change a person's financial future. What they are saying is that by consistently putting money away, letting it make income and leaving that added income in the investment so that you can make money off the income generated allows the profit earned to grow exponentially. Leaving money in investments and not withdrawing profit allows the money to multiply significantly over time.

This process of not touching the principle or the interest of the principle has been compared to a fruit tree. If a fruit tree is productive, the sale of the fruit can be used to plant additional trees and they in turn eventually produce fruit that contains seeds that can be planted to grow even more fruit trees. When trees are cut down they are no longer able to produce fruit but can be used for firewood. It is, therefore, imperative if more trees are to be planted and fruit produced, the current trees be left standing. Taking money away from investments and spending this money removes their opportunity to produce additional profits or fruit.

Investments
There are several basic principles for making wise investment decisions. The first of these is the importance of diversification. Ecclesiastes 11:2 says, *"Give portions to seven, yes to eight, for you do not know what disaster may come upon the land"* (NIV). Investing

in a variety of different types of instruments and in areas that are impacted differently by the natural cycles of the economy provides the safety net described in this Scripture. If one investment does not perform well, it is likely the other investments will provide the stability needed.

To begin developing this kind of diversification, each person will need to determine the amount of risk they are able to tolerate. The person who is willing to take a great deal of risk will invest differently than the person who cringes at the thought of possibly losing some of the money that has been invested. A typical portfolio will contain equities in international markets, some in capital assets, some in large companies, some in small companies and some in very stable investments with a lower return on investment. Mutual funds target a particular market or mix. Some focus on international markets or markets in a particular part of the world. Others mix securities or invest only in certain industries. A mutual fund is a bundle of stocks administered by a manager or a management team. It removes the volatility and risk associated with purchasing an individual stock by allowing investors to spread their investment among a number of stocks.

The seasons of a person's life should impact a persons' investment strategy. According to my broker, 80% of investments should be in stocks when a person is in their twenties and 20% in securities. Stocks represent ownership in a business. If the business does well, the value of the stocks go up. If the business does poorly, the value of the stocks decrease. Securities represent instruments such as bonds that do not represent ownership but money lent to the company by the person holding the bond at a predetermined rate. The risk lies in the potential that the company might not do well and consequently be unable to make the payments owed or, in the worst possible case, pay back the principle when due. As a rule of thumb, people in their thirties, are wise to form a combination of 70% stocks and 30% securities. When in their forties, the combination is 60% stocks and 40% securities, in their fifties, 50% stocks and 50% securities, and in their sixties, 40%

stocks and 60% securities. The principle is that we should make more conservative investments (securities) as we get older. As people age, they have less time to recover any losses incurred from investment in a company that fails. Also keep in mind that each person has a different level of risk tolerance. The person who feels comfortable making high-risk investments, has the potential of making more money, but is at greater risk of loosing his investment. Contemplate what your risk tolerance is and invest in that vein. Do note that the biggest risk is not to invest at all. If you fail to invest, you are guaranteed to make no profit.

Get advice from other people. You have already started gaining advice by reading this book. Additionally, once you have fully reached your goal of three month's wages in an emergency fund, consult a broker or Certified Investment Counselor, listen to television analysts, search the web, read books and articles, and talk with friends who show good judgment with their money management, of course, discuss this with your Accountability Group. Wisdom comes from wise counsel.It may be difficult to know if the advice you receive is good. For this reason, get advice from multiple sources. If one source tells you something that is inconsistent with what everyone else is saying, consider it a red flag. You may also find that initially you won't know what questions to ask about investing. When you listen, read, and learn from a variety of sources, you will be better able to ask the right questions and learn even more.

Saving for Retirement
My friend Leland is a missionary with InFaith. Now his mid-fifties, he anticipates retirement in the coming decade. Unfortunately for Leland, he is one of the 56% of Americans who has not been saving for retirement. When I asked him what he plans to do when it comes time to retire, he was deliberate as he stated contritely, "The Lord will provide." My response was also succinct. "The Lord is providing for you right now so that you can put money way for the future." The Scriptures are clear that wise people store provisions during times of plenty to be used in the future. The illustration is given that just as ants

and other animals store food during the summer so that they can eat in the winter, so we should prepare for the future. Proverbs 5:6-8 reads, *"Go to the ant, you sluggard; consider its ways and be wise! It has no commander, no overseer or ruler, yet it stores its provisions in summer and gathers its food at harvest."* Winter for the ants is a time when no food exists to be harvested. If they had not gathered when food was in abundance they would starve. In the same way, retirement is a time when income and resources for survival are at a minimum. The family who does not prepare for this situation will not do well. It is to a person's advantage to start putting money away early in life, so they can systematically over many years prepare for a comfortable retirement.

Many employers offer to match a certain percentage of what their employees put into their 401(k) retirement plan. For example, if the employee puts $100 into the 401(k), the employer will contribute $100. The total amount that goes into the 401(k) is therefore $200. For the employee, this is free money. Employees who take advantage of this employer match get additional tax-free money. Matching funds are not available from every employer, but any time this or any other matching opportunity is available, it is in the employee's interest to take full advantage of the opportunity.

Many people put off participating in a retirement program because they do not believe they will be able to meet their other financial obligations if they designate money toward a retirement program. Others indicate they will participate once they get out of debt. Neither excuse is valid. Their family budget should be adjusted so at a minimum, they can take advantage of the employer match. If no match exists, money should still be systematically put away for retirement.

The time to begin saving for retirement is now! The longer a person waits, the more must be saved to get the same result later in life. For example, if a person puts $1.00 into a savings plan at the age of 25 it will take $5.00 at the age of 45 to have the same value at the age of 65.

This is due to the compounding power or snowball principle we discussed earlier in this chapter.

The amount of money needed for retirement will be different for each person or family. Consideration of an appropriate life style will dictate the amount of money to be saved. Typically, a person spends much more money at the beginning of retirement than in later years. Initially during the Explorer Phase, time is spent traveling, engaged in hobbies, and social activities. Later, people enter what is called the Hibernation Phase. Time is spent close to home and expenses center around home care and medical issues. Special care should be given when contemplating the amount of money needed to finance the desired lifestyle during the various phases of retirement. Consideration should be given to housing, food, health care, travel, recreation, and other issues in the budget. Once a projected budget for the initial year is complete the amount of money needed annually can be determined. This number, multiplied by 10 (assuming a return on investment of 10%) is the amount needed to be in investments. If $100,000 is needed each year, then at least $1,000,000 should be in investments. Inflation will play a part (average of 3% between 1926 and 2008) but expenses will be less during the Hibernation Phase than during the Explorer Phase. The goal is to not live on the money needed during retirement.

A financially healthy retirement is evidence of wise decisions during a lifetime. Money cannot be saved if it is spent daily at the coffee shop, on overpriced food, clothes that are seldom worn or on interest payments. Follow the advice of the ants and plan now for a healthy financial future.

In Conclusion
The goal of this book has been to get you started in becoming fiscally fit – managing your money in such a way that your finances glorify God and bring your family together. As with physical fitness, financial fitness is an ongoing process. You don't just fix your finances and move onto another area of your life that needs improvement. You must keep in shape financially by living with a new mindset toward money.

A realistic, workable budget is the key to sound personal finance. If you do not have a budget and tell yourself that you simply cannot follow one, experience dictates you are going to have financial difficulties. Your budget must be written so you and others in your family can review it and implement it together.

A budget is a living organism and as such is always changing. Continually revise it, refine it, rework it, and redo it. Your goal is to achieve financial freedom, and you can meet that goal if you continually work at it. It is hard work, but if approached with a positive attitude, it can draw your family together.

You cannot spend more than what you bring in. If you are deficit spending, something is wrong. Follow the snowball plan for debt reduction and get rid of all your debts, making sure you are not incurring more debt as you do so.

Opportunities to save money are all around you. Look for small expenses that can be eliminated or reduced, and you will soon have enough money to meet your larger financial goals. Save and invest money so that you can be your own banker, prepare for the drought years of retirement, and become financially independent.

Above all, keep your priorities right. Remember, *The earth is the Lord's, and everything in it."* We are here to serve him. If we do so, we will be better able to glorify God and enjoy Him forever.

"But thanks be to God! He gives us the victory through our Lord Jesus Christ" (1 Corinthians 15:57, NIV).

Discussion Questions and Assignments:

1. What is the rationale for beginning with a nest egg of $1,000? How is this helpful to a family already in financial trouble?

2. It was recommended that three months, livable income be put aside for the future. What are the benefits of saving this amount of money before making investments?

3. Describe the first three steps to becoming financially independent. How long do you believe it will take you to complete these steps?

4. How much money will you need in order to retire comfortably? Explain the process you used to achieve this number. Indicate your target year for achieving this objective.

5. Explain the concept behind the statement, "Money makes money and the money, money makes, makes money."

6. How did you determine the amount of money you need to put away each month in order to reach your retirement goal?

7. Consider Proverbs 5:6-8. What lessons can we learn from this passage about investments?

8. What is the most important concept you learned from this chapter? Why is this vital to an investment strategy?

9. Explain the impact of Ecclesiastes 11:2 on making wise investments?

10. It has been said that "Everyone should have a plan for becoming a millionaire." Is this a Biblical concept? Is it realistic for you? Explain your rationale.

Period of Years	1%	2%	3%	4%	5%	6%	7%	8%	9%	10%
1	1.0000	1.0000	1.0000	1.0000	1.0000	1.0000	1.0000	1.0000	1.0000	1.0000
2	2.100	2.0200	2.300	2.0400	2.0500	2.0600	2.0700	2,0800	2.0900	2.1000
3	3.0301	3.0604	3.0909	3.1216	3.1525	3.1836	3.2149	3.2464	3.2781	3.3100
4	4.0604	4.1216	4.1836	4.2465	4.3101	4.3746	4.4399	4.5061	4.5731	4.6410
5	5.1010	5.2040	5.3091	5.4163	5.5256	5.6371	5.7507	5.8666	5.9847	6.1051
6	6.1520	6.3081	6.4684	6.6330	6.8019	6.9753	7.1533	7.3359	7.5233	7.7156
7	7.2135	7.4343	7.6625	7.8983	8.1420	8.3938	8.6540	8.9228	9.2004	9.4872
8	8.2857	8.5830	8.8923	8.2142	9.5491	9.8975	10.259	10.636	11.028	11.435
9	9.3685	9.7546	10.159	10.582	11.026	11.491	11.978	12.487	13.021	13.579
10	10.462	10.949	11.463	12.006	12.577	13.180	13.816	14.486	15.192	15.937
11	11.566	12.168	12.807	13.486	14.206	14.971	15.783	16.645	17.560	18.531
12	12.682	13.412	14.192	15.025	15.917	16.869	17.888	18.977	20.140	21.384
13	13.809	14.680	15.617	16.626	17.713	18.882	20.140	21.495	22.953	24.522
14	14.947	15.973	17.086	18.291	19.598	21.051	22.550	24.214	26.019	27.975
15	16.096	17.293	18.598	20.023	21.578	23.276	25.129	27.152	29.360	31.772
16	17.257	18.639	20.156	21.824	23.657	25.672	27.888	30.324	33.003	34.949
17	18.430	20.012	21.761	23.697	25.840	28.212	30.840	33.750	36.973	40.544
18	19.614	21.412	23.414	25.645	28.132	30.905	33.999	37.450	41.301	45.599
19	20.810	22.840	25.116	27.671	30.539	33.760	37.379	41.446	46.018	51.159
20	22.019	24.297	26.870	29.778	33.066	36.785	40.995	45.762	51.160	57.275
21	23.239	25.783	28.783	31.969	35.719	39.992	44.865	50.422	56.764	64.002
22	24.471	27.299	30.536	34.248	38.505	43.392	49.005	55.456	62.873	71.402
23	25.716	28.845	32.452	36.617	41.430	46.995	53.436	60.893	69.531	79.543
24	26.973	30.421	34.426	39.082	44.502	50.815	58.176	66.764	76.789	88.497
25	28.243	32.030	36.459	41.645	47.727	54.864	63.249	73.105	84.700	98.347
26	29.525	33.670	38.553	44.311	51.113	59.156	68.676	79.954	93.323	109.18
27	30.820	35.344	40.709	47.084	54.669	63.705	74.483	87.350	102.72	121.09
28	32.129	37.051	42.930	49.967	58.402	68.528	80.697	95.338	112.96	134.20
29	33.450	38.792	45.218	52.966	62.322	73.639	87.346	103.96	124.13	148.63
30	34.784	40.568	47.575	56.084	66.438	79.058	94.460	113.28	136.30	164.49
40	48.886	60.402	75.401	95.025	120.79	154.76	199.63	259.05	337.88	442.59
50	64.463	84.579	112.79	152.66	209.34	290.33	406.52	573.76	815.08	1163.9
60	81.669	114.05	163.05	237.99	353.58	533.12	813.52	1253.2	1944.7	3034.8

Period of Years	12%	14%	15%	16%	18%	20%	24%	28%	32%	36%
1	1.0000	1.0000	1.0000	1.0000	1.0000	1.0000	1.0000	1.0000	1.0000	1.0000
2	2.1200	2.1400	2.1500	2.1600	2.1800	2.2000	2.2400	2.2800	2.3200	2.3600
3	3.3744	3.4396	3.4725	3.5056	3.5724	3.6400	3.7776	3.9184	4.0624	4.2096
4	4.7793	4.9211	4.9934	5.0665	5.2154	5.3680	5.6842	6.0156	6.3624	6.7251
5	6.3528	6.6101	6.7424	6.8771	7.1542	7.4416	8.0484	8.6999	9.3983	10.146
6	8.1152	8.5355	8.7537	8.9775	9.4420	9.9299	10.980	12.135	13.405	14.798
7	10.089	10.730	11.066	11.413	12.141	12.915	14.615	16.533	18.695	21.126
8	12.299	13.232	13.726	14.240	15.327	16.499	19.122	22.163	25.678	29.731
9	14.775	16.085	16.785	17.518	19.085	20.798	24.712	29.369	34.895	41.435
10	17.548	19.337	20.303	21.321	23.521	25.958	31.634	38.592	47.061	57.351
11	20.654	23.044	24.349	25.732	28.755	32.150	40.237	50.398	63.121	78.998
12	24.133	27.270	29.001	30.850	34.931	39.580	50.894	65.510	84.320	108.43
13	28.029	32.088	34.351	36.786	42.218	48.496	64.109	84.852	112.30	148.47
14	32.392	37.581	40.504	43.672	50.818	59.195	80.496	109.61	149.23	202.92
15	37.279	43.842	47.580	51.659	60.965	72.035	100.81	141.30	197.99	276.97
16	42.753	50.980	55.717	60.925	72.939	87.442	126.04	181.86	262.35	377.69
17	48.883	59.117	65.075	71.673	87.068	105.93	157.25	233.79	347.30	514.66
18	55.749	68.394	75.394	84.140	103.74	128.11	195.99	300.25	459.44	700.93
19	63.439	78.969	88.211	98.603	123.41	154.74	244.03	385.32	607.47	954.27
20	72.052	91.042	102.44	115.37	146.62	186.68	303.60	494.21	802.86	1298.8
21	81.698	104.76	118.81	134.84	174.02	225.02	377.46	633.59	1060.7	1767.3
22	92.502	120.43	137.63	157.41	206.34	271.03	469.05	811.99	1401.2	2404.6
23	104.60	138.29	159.27	183.60	244.48	326.23	582.62	1040.3	1850.6	3271.3
24	118.15	158.65	184.16	213.97	289.49	392.48	723.46	1332.6	2443.8	4449.9
25	133.33	181.87	212.79	249.21	342.60	471.98	898.09	1706.8	3226.8	6052.9
26	150.33	208.33	245.71	290.08	405.27	567.37	1114.6	2185.7	4260.4	8233.0
27	169.37	238.49	283.56	337.50	479.22	681.85	1383.1	2798.7	5624.7	11197.9
28	190.69	272.88	327.10	392.50	566.48	819.22	1716.0	3583.3	7425.6	15230.2
29	214.58	312.09	377.16	456.30	669.44	964.06	2128.9	4587.6	9802.9	20714.1
30	241.33	356.78	434.74	530.31	790.94	1181.8	2640.9	5873.2	12940.	28172.2
40	767.09	1342.0	1779.0	2360.7	4163.2	7343.8	22728.	69377.	*	*
50	2400.0	4994.5	7217.7	10435.	21813.	45497.	*	*	*	*
60	7471.6	18535.	29219.	46057.	*	*	*	*	*	*

CPSIA information can be obtained at www.ICGtesting.com
·Printed in the USA
BVOW061010100912

299937BV00002B/1/P